S0-BCQ-947

the Healthy Heart Cookbook

©1999 Affinity Communication Corp. and Bristol Publishing Enterprises, Inc., P.O. Box 1737, San Leandro, California 94577. World rights reserved. No part of this publication may be reproduced in any form, nor may it be stored in a retrieval system, transmitted, or otherwise copied for public or private use without prior written permission from the publisher.

ISBN 1-55867-236

Printed in Singapore through Global Interprint.

design: Shanti L. Nelson
photography: Lisa Keenan
cover food stylist: Susan Devaty
cover photo: John A. Benson
project editor: Lisa M. Tooker

the Healthy Heart Cookbook

indulge your palate – improve your health

Brenda D. Adderly, M.H.A. and Catherine Pagano Fulde

BRISTOL PUBLISHING ENTERPRISES
San Leandro, California

CONTENTS

THE HEALTHY HEART

RECIPES FOR A HEALTHY HEART

heart disease & hypertension

HEART DISEASE & HYPERTENSION

THE HEART AND VASCULAR SYSTEM is one of the largest and most important systems in our bodies. Its function is to deliver oxygen and vital nutrition to cells throughout the body and to aid in the removal of cellular waste products. To achieve this goal, our hearts beat an average of 100,000 times per day, pumping 2,500 to 5,000 gallons of blood through 60,000 miles of blood vessels. The heart will beat 2.5 billion times and pump 100,000 million gallons of blood in the average lifetime.

Even though a healthy heart is so vital to our existence, many of us suffer from heart and blood vessel diseases. More than 60 million Americans suffer from these conditions and in 1993, 42% (950,000 people) of all deaths in the U.S. were caused by heart and blood vessel disease. These diseases are often referred to as the "silent killers" because the first symptom or sign of illness, in many cases, is a fatal heart attack. Heart and blood vessel diseases and hypertension are the main causes of heart attacks, yet these conditions can be controlled and in some cases, reversed by maintaining a healthy diet and lifestyle.

HEART DISEASE

THERE ARE MANY FORMS OF HEART DISEASE; however, this term is most often used to describe a particular disease of the heart's blood vessels known as atherosclerosis — a hardening of the artery walls. These blood vessels, which are also known as coronary arteries, supply oxygen and vital nutrients to the heart. Over time, the inner walls of the arteries become clogged with a buildup of cellular debris, fat and cholesterol. This buildup is called plaque. When plaque clogs arteries, blood clots form and less blood is able to get through to the heart. Yet, about 90% of the artery is blocked before symptoms of atherosclerosis are noticeable. When the blood flow is severely restricted or blocked, damage to the heart muscle occurs and results in a heart attack. If the blood supply is restricted for a long time, heart muscle cells suffer irreversible damage and die. Disability or death can result, depending on how much of the heart muscle is damaged.

HYPERTENSION

COUPLED WITH HEART DISEASE, the other major condition that can bring on heart attacks is high blood pressure. High blood pressure, which is also referred to as hypertension, means the pressure in your arteries is consistently above the normal range. The control of blood pressure in our bodies involves very sophisticated and complex checks and balances. A blood pressure reading represents the amount of blood that is pumped out by the heart and then into the blood vessels.

Your blood pressure reading is written as 2 numbers, such as 122/78 millimeters of mercury (mm Hg). The top, systolic number is the pressure when the heart beats. The bottom, diastolic number is the pressure when the heart is at rest. High blood pressure is a consistently elevated pressure of 140 systolic or higher and/or 90 diastolic or higher. The great danger is that you often don't know if you have high blood pressure. You don't feel sick and there are no visible signs. The only way to know for sure is to see a doctor. High blood pressure, like atherosclerosis, can lead to hardened arteries and heart attacks, among other serious health concerns.

HEART DISEASE
traditional *risk factors*

WITH HEART DISEASE as the number 1 killer in the United States, the causes for the disease are well known. The major heart disease risk factors are:

- high blood pressure
- high cholesterol
- obesity and diabetes
- smoking
- family history of early heart disease
- lack of physical activity

THE RISK OF HEART DISEASE CAN BE GREATLY REDUCED by eliminating the various factors associated with premature death from these conditions. When 1 or more of these factors are present, the risk of heart attack increases dramatically. And as additional risk factors are added to the mix, risk rises at even more alarming rates:

presence of one of the major risk factors	**30%** *increased risk*
high cholesterol and high blood pressure	**300%** *increased risk*
high cholesterol and smoking	**350%** *increased risk*
high blood pressure and smoking	**350%** *increased risk*
smoking, high blood cholesterol, and high blood pressure	**720%** *increased risk*

HIGH BLOOD PRESSURE

HYPERTENSION PLAGUES 50 MILLION AMERICANS; however, 80% of them are in the borderline to moderate range. According to the American Heart Association, 3 major factors that contribute to hypertension are lack of exercise, obesity and excessive alcohol consumption. Since high blood pressure is a significant risk factor for heart disease, as well as strokes, it is important that patients try to control the condition. Yet, more than 50% of patients with hypertension are not working to bring their blood pressure down. Hypertension tends to be aggravated by smoking, high salt intake and obesity. By controlling these factors, blood pressure levels have been shown to decrease significantly within 6 months to 1 year without medication.

HIGH BLOOD CHOLESTEROL LEVELS

THERE IS NO DISPUTE AMONG SCIENTISTS that elevated levels of cholesterol in the blood increase the risk of death due to heart disease. The problem with cholesterol is that it's a fat and it doesn't dissolve in the bloodstream. That means elevated amounts of cholesterol can accumulate and form plaque that clogs arteries and leads to artherosclerosis. Cholesterol is an essential chemical in our bodies. It is used in the synthesis of hormones like estrogen and testosterone and it is necessary for the formation of cell membranes.

Cholesterol cells circulate in the bloodstream in complexes called "lipoproteins" containing triglycerides (another type of fat), phospholipids (mostly lecithin) and proteins. Lipoproteins act as carrier proteins, transporting cholesterol cells through our blood. There are 2 major types of lipoproteins — low-density lipoproteins (LDLs) and high-density lipoproteins (HDLs). LDLs are associated with a high risk of developing atherosclerosis, as they are responsible for transporting fats in the form of triglycerides and cholesterol from the liver to body cells. HDLs, on the other hand, return fats to the liver and an abundance of HDLs is associated with a lower risk of heart disease.

The measure most commonly used to gauge cholesterol gives us a reading for the total amount of cholesterol in the blood. The current recommendation is that the reading should be less than 200 milligrams per deciliter of blood (mg/dl). Yet, in addition to the overall reading, one should also look at individual readings for LDL and HDL cholesterol. The HDL cholesterol level should be greater than 35 mg/dl. There are two separate readings for LDLs. One covers LDL cholesterol and the other covers LDL triglycerides. The level of LDL cholesterol should be less than 130 mg/dl and the level of LDL triglycerides should be less than 150 mg/dl. It has been shown that the risk of heart disease drops dramatically as the level of LDLs is decreased, while those of HDLs are increased.

Although in most cases, high cholesterol can be attributed to lifestyle and dietary factors, elevations can also be due to genetic factors. There are several inherited disorders that can elevate cholesterol levels in the blood. With these disorders, the LDL cholesterol receptor is damaged and one's body overproduces LDL cholesterol. This same type of damage can also occur with patients who have diabetes and with aging in general. Elevated cholesterol levels can also be caused by low thyroid function. Individuals with this condition are prone to heart disease because of an increased LDL cholesterol level and a decreased HDL cholesterol level.

LDL/HDL CHOLESTEROL LEVELS REALLY MATTER

For every 1% drop in the LDL cholesterol level, the risk of a heart attack drops by 2%. And, for every 1% increase in HDL cholesterol levels, the risk of heart attack drops 3 to 4 percent.

DIABETES & OBESITY

DIABETES ALSO PLAYS A PROMINENT ROLE as a major risk factor for heart disease, and in turn, heart attacks. Diabetes is the inability of the body to produce or respond to insulin needs properly. Insulin is the compound that allows the body to use glucose — sugar. There are 2 types of diabetes and Type II (adult) is often associated with obesity. This type can be delayed or controlled with diet and exercise. Diabetics are at 2 to 3 times the risk of nondiabetics of dying prematurely from atherosclerosis. Many adults in our society develop Type II diabetes because they consume a lot of food and don't exercise much. Over half of all Americans are overweight. Of people between the ages of 50 and 60, 64% of women and 73% of men are identified as overweight. In addition to causing diabetes, obesity also raises cholesterol and triglyceride levels, raises blood pressure and lowers HDL cholesterol levels. The main causes of obesity are the consumption of too many calories and lack of exercise. The American Heart Association (AHA) defines obesity as follows: "when body weight exceeds 'desirable' weight for height and gender by 20% or more and when the excess weight is fat rather than water, muscle or bone."

SMOKING

THE U.S. SURGEON GENERAL has identified cigarette smoking as the most important risk factor for coronary heart disease. The statistics show that smokers have 3 to 5 times the risk of coronary artery disease as nonsmokers.

HOW SMOKING EFFECTS THE CARDIOVASCULAR SYSTEM

Studies have demonstrated that smoking actually affects the progression of atherosclerosis in the blood vessels, but if you quit smoking, your risk of developing the disease goes down to that of a nonsmoker within only 1 to 2 years. Scientists have identified more than 4,000 chemicals that are carried in cigarette smoke and at least 50 of these are known carcinogens. These chemicals are especially hard on the cardiovascular system. They travel through the bloodstream by attaching to LDL cholesterol molecules. Once attached, they either damage the cholesterol molecules, which in turn damage the artery linings, or they damage the linings directly. If you have a high cholesterol level and you smoke, the damage is even greater, because more toxins are carried through your bloodstream. In addition to heart disease, smoking has other detrimental effects on the cardiovascular system, such as contributing to high blood pressure.

The Effects of Passive Smoke on the Cardiovascular System

NUMEROUS STUDIES HAVE PROVEN that even passive smoke inhaled by nonsmokers is very damaging. Scientists have found that secondhand smoke reduces a person's oxygen supply, damages arteries, lowers the "good" HDL cholesterol and increases the risk of blood clotting. Although the precise causes for its damaging effects on the cardiovascular system are not completely understood, physicians believe that nonsmokers may be more sensitive to smoke and that secondhand smoke is more toxic. Nonsmokers who have been exposed to passive smoke for extended periods of time have displayed symptoms similar to smokers. There is damage to the lining of their arteries and their exercise capacity is extremely limited. In this country, more than 37,000 coronary heart disease deaths each year are attributed to secondhand smoke.

Family History of Early Heart Disease

RESEARCHERS KNOW that heart disease tends to run in families and that if it develops at a relatively young age in parents, it may also develop in children. The major risk factors discussed are usually present in these cases. If the adults in a family are obese and develop heart disease, there is a good chance that the children will also be obese and will then develop heart disease later in life.

nutrit

THE ROLE OF NUTRITION
in preventing *heart disease & hypertension*

YOUR DIET PLAYS A PIVOTAL ROLE in preventing or managing heart disease and hypertension. Even after other lifestyle factors such as smoking, exercise and weight loss are taken into account, the food you eat is one of the most important factors in predicting who will develop atherosclerosis. Since clogged arteries are caused by a buildup of cholesterol and cholesterol comes from one's diet, managing what you eat can in many cases have a significant impact on whether or not you develop heart disease. Even though family history does play a role, everyone can have some influence on the health of his or her heart and cardiovascular systems through diet. And, physicians have found that it's never too late to begin eating healthier foods. If atherosclerosis has already set in, changing one's diet will prevent it from progressing. If one has already had a heart attack, diet is a key factor to living a healthy, productive life after the event. Proper diet has been shown to reverse atherosclerosis and help restore the blood vessels to a healthier state. For those lucky enough not to have heart disease, diet is vital to steering clear of atherosclerosis.

The right foods help to keep the blood vessels free and clear and also prevent the blood from clotting. These choice foods can combat the buildup of cholesterol and other blood fats. The efficacy of a low-fat, healthy-heart diet has been confirmed by numerous studies of various peoples throughout the world. By looking at incidences of heart disease and correlating them with diet, researchers have been able to construct an accurate picture of the foods we should eat and those we should stay away from to avoid heart disease.

preve

EAT FRUITS & VEGETABLES EAT LESS RED MEAT & DAIRY NOT

ALL FATS ARE BAD EAT MORE GRAINS & FIBER ENJOY

MEALS WITH WINE BE SURE TO CONSUME ENOUGH WATER

SOLUBLE FIBERS MAKE ANTIOXIDANTS A MAJOR COMPO-

NENT OF YOUR DIET

SO, HOW DOES ONE go about constructing a heart disease prevention diet? The basic approach should be to eat a balanced diet. A balanced diet eaten on a regular basis that is low-fat, low cholesterol and includes soluble fibers has been shown to lower blood cholesterol. Achieving this goal can be tricky in our fast food culture. The major challenge to a better diet is usually inconvenience. Snacks and processed foods are much easier to grab on the run as compared to fruits and vegetables, which require preparation and refrigeration. Getting enough fiber is also tricky. The U.S. Surgeon General and other health organizations recommend 25 to 35 grams of fiber per day. The typical American diet, which is high in processed foods, only includes about 10 to 12 grams of fiber per day. To get the recommended 25 to 35 grams of fiber per day, many individuals need to take supplements. High fiber supplements should be low calorie, from multiple fiber sources and contain no saturated fats. Many people also choose processed and fast foods because they are cheaper than their healthier alternatives, but when you are aiming to prolong your life, the extra cost is well worth it. Keep in mind that many foods that are healthy for our hearts can be cooked at home and so the overall cost may actually be less than eating prepared foods in restaurants and fast food establishments. Other important elements of a heart disease prevention diet are the consumption of antioxidants and other nutritional supplements as defenses against heart disease before aggressive interventions with surgery and drugs are needed.

USE FATS AND OILS SPARINGLY AND STICK TO THOSE THAT ARE LOWEST IN SATURATED FATTY ACIDS AND CHOLESTEROL, SUCH AS CANOLA, OLIVE, SAFFLOWER AND PEANUT OILS. REMEMBER THAT EVEN THOUGH COCONUT OIL, PALM OIL AND PALM KERNEL OIL ARE VEGETABLE OILS AND HAVE NO CHOLESTEROL, THEY ARE HIGH IN SATURATED FATTY ACIDS. WHEN COOKING, CHOOSE STYLES THAT ADD LITTLE OR NO FAT TO THE FOOD. BE SURE TO ASK FOR LOW-FAT PREPARATIONS WHEN EATING OUT.

oils&

FATS AND CHOLESTEROL

Foods that have high concentrations of animal fat and some foods with vegetable fats are the main sources of dietary cholesterol. There are 3 main types of fat — *saturated, hydrogenated* and *monounsaturated*. Those that raise cholesterol levels and should be avoided are saturated fatty acids and hydrogenated fats. Monounsaturated fats, on the other hand, are good for you.

SATURATED FATTY ACIDS

SATURATED FATTY ACIDS are easily identified because they are usually solid at room temperature. This form of fat is the main dietary culprit in raising blood cholesterol levels. These fats are found in foods from animals and some plants. Foods that have high amounts of saturated fatty acids include beef, beef fat, veal, lamb, pork, lard, poultry fat, butter, cream cheese, milk and other dairy products made from whole milk. These foods also contain dietary cholesterol.

Foods from plants that contain high concentrations of saturated fatty acids include coconut oil, palm oil, cocoa butter and palm kernel oil (sometimes called tropical oils).

HYDROGENATED FATS

FOODS THAT ARE PROCESSED often contain fats that have undergone a chemical process known as hydrogenation. Hydrogenate means to add hydrogen, which in the case of fatty acids means to saturate. This process changes a liquid oil, which is naturally high in unsaturated fatty acids, to a more solid and saturated form. The more a fat is hydrogenated, the more saturated it becomes. Many commercial, processed foods contain hydrogenated or partially hydrogenated vegetable oils. Studies have shown that these types of fats may raise blood cholesterol.

MONOUNSATURATED & POLYUNSATURATED FATS

MONOUNSATURATED AND POLYUNSATURATED FATS lower cholesterol levels when substituted for saturated fats. Monounsaturated fats are preferable to polyunsaturated because they reduce the bad LDL cholesterol levels without endangering levels of "good" HDL cholesterol. Polyunsaturated fats on the other hand reduce the overall blood cholesterol levels of both LDL and HDL cholesterol. However, both types of fats are preferable to saturated or hydrogenated fats. Monounsaturated fats are especially high in oils such as olive, canola and peanut oil. Polyunsaturated fats, which remain liquid at room temperature, are found mainly in plant products such as safflower, sunflower, corn and soybean oils as well as in fish.

ANIMAL FATS

IT IS A WELL-ESTABLISHED FACT that the populations that eat the most animal fats have the highest rates of heart disease. Animal fat has been referred to as the dietary demon for coronary artery disease. We know that animal fat raises blood cholesterol, which destroys arteries, it encourages blood stickiness and it suppresses the blood's clot-dissolving mechanisms. Americans and other Westerners who consume 15 to 20 percent of their total calorie intake in the form of animal fat have the highest rates of heart disease in the world.

Reducing animal fats from your diet can help to unclog arteries, so it's never too late to make the switch. Studies have shown that restrictions in animal fat consumption can help block formation and growth of fatty plaque in the arteries and may even help to shrink plaque that is already formed.

DIET RECOMMENDATIONS FOR

Optimal Cardiovascular Health

consume less saturated fat and cholesterol by reducing animal products in your diet.

eat large amounts of fiber-rich plant foods, such as fruits, vegetables, raw nuts, seeds, grains and legumes.

drink a minimum of 48 ounces of water each day.

drink as little coffee as possible, both caffeinated and decaffeinated.

THE ROLE OF ANTIOXIDANTS

OXIDANTS OR "FREE RADICALS" have been linked to cancer, high blood pressure, heart disease, atherosclerosis, stroke, cataracts, asthma and Parkinson's disease, to name a few. Free radicals or oxidants are unstable molecules. They are thought to have come from such sources as tobacco smoke, air pollutants, organic solvents, anesthetics, pesticides, certain medications and radiation.

Antioxidants are vitamins acting in conjunction with minerals that help to neutralize free radicals before they can damage the body. Our bodies do not manufacture antioxidants so they must come from our diet. It is important for vitamins and minerals that are taken as antioxidants to supplement a diet, to be balanced in synergistic combinations. Although we know that LDL cholesterol is linked to heart disease, the connection is actually more precise than first recognized. The true LDL cholesterol culprits for heart disease are those that have been oxidized. Normal, unoxidized LDL is not in itself directly associated with heart disease. Thus, a cardiac-disease prevention program should have two goals:

cardiac prevention program

two goals | lower LDL cholesterol to safe levels

prevent the LDL that is present from being oxidized

EXPERIMENTS HAVE SHOWN that antioxidants such as vitamin C, vitamin E and beta carotene can prevent LDL cholesterol from oxidizing in the laboratory. Because of these studies, many believe that these vitamins could decrease the risk of heart disease, preventing LDL oxidation in the bloodstream. A diet aimed at lowering the risk of heart disease should include lots of foods that contain vitamins C and E.

vitam

VITAMIN C IS THE BODY'S most important antioxidant. It plays an important role in preventing heart disease. In addition, it also strengthens the collagen structures of the arteries, lowers the overall cholesterol level and blood pressure and raises HDL cholesterol levels. Even in studies with smokers, vitamin C has shown to be very effective in preventing LDL cholesterol from oxidizing. Researchers found that vitamin C helps to absorb some of the damaging chemicals (called free radicals) in cigarette smoke that cause damage to the arterial wall.

foods

high in vitamin

sweet red pepper
cantaloupe
pimientos
strawberries
papaya
brussels sprouts
kiwi fruit
tomatoes
oranges

high in vitamin

sunflower seeds
walnuts
almonds
hazelnuts
cashews
wheat germ
soybeans
rice & wheat bran

SELENIUM

THE TRACE MINERAL SELENIUM is an antioxidant that has been shown to play a role in heart disease. Low selenium levels are linked to a decreased risk for cardiovascular disease, as well as cancer and premature aging. Selenium supplementation increases the ratio of HDL to LDL cholesterol. It appears to offer protection to smokers more than any other group.

SELENIUM IN FOODS   Each of the foods listed contains the same amount of selenium as a 100-microgram pill.

- 5 ounces chicken livers
- 8 ounces dry oat bran
- 1 Brazil nut
- 4 ounces canned light tuna
- 5 ounces cooked oysters
- 5 cups puffed wheat cereal
- 4 ounces sunflower seeds

CHOLESTEROL & DIET

SINCE WE KNOW THAT CHOLESTEROL is the main culprit in atherosclerosis, we should eat foods that keep bad cholesterols to a minimum. Since there are several types of cholesterol, some of which are good for us like HDL cholesterol and others that are not, such as LDL cholesterol and triglycerides, a beneficial diet must take into account each food's effect on these different types of cholesterol. Diets that control bad cholesterol have been shown to dramatically slow the progression of atherosclerosis by 50 to 70% and even help reverse existing artery clogging by shrinking plaque on artery walls.

A healthy heart diet will increase the amount of HDL cholesterol and reduce as much as possible LDL cholesterol.

fruits
&
vegetables

THE BEST PRESCRIPTION

A DIET RICH IN FRUITS AND VEGETABLES has proven to be most effective in cutting heart disease risk. Fruits and vegetables are high in fiber and contain antioxidants that prevent LDL cholesterol from forming plaque in the arteries. Fiber is believed to prevent cholesterol from even reaching the bloodstream, since it is able to absorb fats in the digestive tract. One healthy approach is to become a vegetarian; however, this may not be a choice for many. Vegetarians who avoid all animal products have lower cholesterol and LDL levels and lower rates of heart disease, high blood pressure, obesity and diabetes. For those who choose not to eliminate animal-based products altogether, a more realistic goal would be to reduce intake from animal fat as much as possible. The best compromise is to have 1 meat-free meal every day. It's important to closely monitor protein intake, since it might be lowered when meat is cut out of your diet. Skim and fat-free dairy products are excellent sources of calcium and protein that should be included in your diet to make up for the protein shortfall. Various plant-based proteins can be combined in the following combinations, so that your body receives all the amino acids it needs to make protein for muscles and other functions:

GRAINS   combine rice with low-fat cheese, legumes or sesame
combine wheat with legumes or peanuts and fat-free milk
combine corn with legumes

LEGUMES   combine beans with wheat or corn
combine soybeans with rice and wheat, corn and fat-free milk
combine wheat and sesame or peanuts and sesame

NUTS &
SEEDS   combine sesame with beans, peanuts, or soybeans and wheat
combine peanuts with sunflower seeds

NUTRITION, SALT & HYPERTENSION

SINCE HYPERTENSION GREATLY INCREASES heart disease risk, managing this condition should be a priority for everyone who suffers from its symptoms. For most patients, diet alterations can lower blood pressure significantly. The key dietary approaches that can improve hypertension are cutting down on salt, drinking alcohol in moderation and eating more fruits and vegetables. Salt should be avoided by those suffering from hypertension because large concentrations of it in the bloodstream may cause the blood plasma to absorb water, thus creating blood volume and consequently blood pressure. Hypertension is common in individuals who are overweight, so healthy eating to lose weight also should improve hypertension.

Since blood pressure is a major marker of heart health, keeping it normal — not in excess of 140/90 — will help to protect against heart attack and strokes. There are many foods one can eat that are known to lower blood pressure quite effectively.

foods &
nutrients

that can *reduce*
high blood pressure

POTASSIUM SEVERAL RECENT STUDIES HAVE SHOWN THAT POTASSIUM supplementation can lower blood pressure for people with hypertension. Scientists found that not only did potassium lower blood pressure in patients with hypertension, it also aided in preventing the onset of hypertension by lowering blood pressure levels. Notably, potassium lowered blood pressure by a greater degree among patients who were unable to lower their salt intake, so it is especially recommended for salt users. This study was conducted with potassium in capsule form; however, it is also possible to obtain potassium through diet. Many fruits and vegetables, particularly citrus fruits and bananas, contain high concentrations of potassium. In fact, eating 5 or 6 fruits a day high in potassium achieves the same result as a supplement.

foods high in
potassium

potatoes
cantaloupe
avocado
beet greens
peaches
prunes
tomato juice
yogurt
lima beans
salmon
banana
acorn squash

CALCIUM

ALTHOUGH CALCIUM IS not believed to lower blood pressure in everyone, experiments have shown that calcium can help to lower blood pressure for some individuals. Maintaining adequate calcium consumption from dietary sources for people under 40 may even prevent them from developing high blood pressure at a later stage in life.

sources of calcium

ricotta cheese

Parmesan cheese

milk

mackerel

yogurt

salmon

sardines

collards

turnip greens

kale

broccoli

CELERY
can work *blood pressure miracles*

PRACTITIONERS OF CHINESE MEDICINE have known about the benefits of celery for hundreds of years. It contains compounds that can lower blood pressure within a matter of weeks when just 2 to 4 stalks a day are eaten. The compound that gives celery its aroma is also the one that seems to be responsible for its cholesterol-lowering power. Researchers who have studied celery's blood pressure-lowering ability believe that it works by reducing blood concentrations of stress hormones that cause blood vessels to constrict. So, it should be most effective in individuals whose high blood pressure is caused by stress. Since about half of all hypertension cases in the United States are linked to stress, these are the cases in which celery may prove to be beneficial for combating high blood pressure.

FRUITS & VEGETABLES
curb high *blood pressure*

AGENTS IN FRUITS AND VEGETABLES seem to be powerful blood pressure reducers. Although researchers have not found a particular compound responsible for lowering blood pressure, they believe it may be the high fiber content in fruit or the antioxidant properties in both fruits and vegetables. Regardless of the fact that the specific agent has not been found, we know that diets high in fruits and vegetables will lower blood pressure.

COFFEE

& high *blood pressure*

ALTHOUGH COFFEE HAS been shown to raise blood pressure levels temporarily, it has not been proven that it can have lasting effects on blood pressure. It seems to be most harmful for people under a lot of stress. Stress combined with caffeine, both caffeinated and decaffeinated, raises blood pressure to higher levels than stress alone. For this reason, those who have high blood pressure and tend to be under a lot of stress should drink coffee in moderation.

foods
for a
healthy
heart

HEALTHY HEART FOODS

SINCE OUR DIETARY GOALS should now be clear, we can now look at the foods that will best accomplish these goals. There are many tasty and varied foods that one can turn to for a rich and interesting healthy diet. For some who are used to eating processed and fast foods, it might take quite an effort to make the transition. However, these foods will not only help keep cholesterol levels low, they'll also help in maintaining ideal weight and provide all of the essential nutrients, vitamins and minerals needed for our bodies to function at their optimal level.

FISH   It is well known that seafood eaters around the world have lower heart disease rates than Americans. Even eating very small amounts of fish can have a positive effect. A study in the Netherlands showed that eating just 1 ounce of fish could cut the chances of heart disease in half. It is believed that the key ingredient in fish is its unique fat, which has the capability to break down cholesterol.

For individuals who have already had a heart attack, one of the most effective ways they can prevent another attack is to turn to a high fish diet. Not only will fish prevent heart attacks, it will also help in keeping arteries clear for those who have already had heart surgery. Patients who ate more than 8 ounces of seafood per week were about half as apt to suffer reclogging as those who ate much less fish.

Fish that are best for combating heart disease are oily, such as sardines, mackerel or salmon.

fish oil
fights heart disease by:

reducing blood vessel constriction

increasing blood flow

increasing blood clot-dissolving activity

lowering triglyceride levels

raising HDL cholesterol levels

making cell membranes more flexible

lowering blood pressure

OLIVE OIL

OLIVE OIL   We have known for years that heart disease is much lower in Mediterranean countries that use olive oil-based products. Even though diets in Greece, Spain, Italy and Southern France are high in fat, most of the fat comes from olive oil and other olive oil-type fats, rather than from animal fats. Heart disease rates as well as cancer rates in the Mediterranean are so low that olive oil is sometimes called the longevity food.

The difference between olive oil fat and other types of animal fats that are harmful is that olive oil contains monounsaturated fats, whereas animal fat is saturated. Monounsaturated fat is easier on the arteries than saturated fat. It lowers bad LDL cholesterol but leaves HDL good cholesterol as it is. Monounsaturated fats also contain antioxidants that fight against artery damage from LDL cholesterol.

A COMPARISON OF THE MEDITERRANEAN & AMERICAN DIETS

In order for the American diet to more closely resemble a Mediterranean diet, big changes are needed:

eat double the amount of seafood

increase vegetable intake by 66 percent and fruit by 10%

eat 45% less red meat

consume 4 times as much olive oil

cut down on other vegetable oils by as much as 50%

cut down on whole milk, cream and butterfat by 50%

consume 16% fewer eggs

eat 20% more whole grains and beans

NUTS   Eating a few nuts a day has proven to be an effective antidote to heart disease. This might be hard to believe, but nuts are rich in fiber and olive oil-type fats. Some people avoid nuts because of their high fat content. If weight loss is an issue, then cutting out nuts might make sense. But the fat in nuts is monounsaturated and this kind of fat is not bad for you, unlike animal fat. Nuts also contain antioxidants, such as vitamin E, which can guard against cholesterol buildup in the arteries. The nuts that are the most effective are almonds and walnuts. Oil extracted from almonds is chemically identical to that found in olive oil. Thus, if olive oil is good for the heart, so is almond oil. Research showed that patients on low-fat diets who ate 2 ounces of walnuts a day were able to drop their cholesterol levels by an average of 18% after 2 months. Eating nuts each day as a substitute for other sources of fat and calories is a great way to improve cholesterol levels.

foods that contain fat & protect the arteries

hazelnuts

avocados

olive oil

almonds

canola oil

BEANS
Beans of any variety rate near the top of the scale among foods that will effectively lower LDL cholesterol and raise HDL cholesterol. All types of beans including chickpeas, lentils, soybeans, kidney, navy, black, pintos and baked beans have been shown to lower LDL cholesterol levels by as much as 20%, by eating 1 cup a day. Beans also drive up HDL cholesterol by 9% a day on average; however, this effect does not happen quickly. It has been observed among those who have eaten large portions of beans for more than 1 year.

OATS, OATMEAL & OAT BRAN
A large bowl of oatmeal in the morning or a medium-sized bowl of oat bran cereal has lowered bad cholesterol in nearly all the studies carried out with this food. It is interesting to note that the cholesterol-lowering effect was observed when only 2 ounces of oat bran were eaten. Larger amounts of oat bran didn't increase its efficacy. You need about twice as much oatmeal as oat bran to achieve the same result. Oats are believed to be effective in cutting bad cholesterol because they contain a gummy fiber that forms a gel in the intestinal tract. This gel interferes with the absorption and production of cholesterol, so that more cholesterol is removed from the bloodstream.

GARLIC

Among garlic's many health benefits, it has also been shown to lower blood pressure and cholesterol levels. Garlic contains several volatile compounds and it is these substances that are generally considered responsible for its efficacy with respect to heart disease. The same compound that is responsible for its pungent odor — allicin — is also the compound for which we attribute its pharmacological properties. Allicin is much stronger in its raw form — when garlic is cooked it loses much of its overpowering smell as well as its powerful pharmacological effects. Since there are very few among us who relish the thought of eating raw garlic cloves, manufacturers have developed commercial forms of garlic that have the full benefits of the clove without the strong smell and taste. Yet in terms of cooking, the aim should be to increase the use of fresh garlic as much as possible. If individuals ingest large amounts of fresh garlic in their diets, supplementation may not be necessary, as demonstrated in a study done in India. Garlic was a main staple of those in the study, and tests showed that those who consumed the largest amounts had the most favorable blood cholesterol readings.

ONIONS   One of the most effective HDL cholesterol boosters is raw onion. Studies have shown that half a raw onion or its equivalent in juice is capable of raising HDL cholesterol an average of 30% in most people with heart disease or cholesterol problems. Although eating half a raw onion each day may be more than some people can bear, even smaller amounts are beneficial. Cooked onions do not have the same HDL cholesterol-raising ability; however, they are beneficial in fighting heart disease in other ways.

AVOCADOS

Avocados contain fats similar to those found in olive oil and almonds and have the same cholesterol-lowering abilities. Even though avocados do contain a lot of fat, monounsaturated fat is not bad for you. Tests in Australia and Israel have shown that eating ½ to 1½ raw avocados per day lowers LDL cholesterol levels by as much as 8%. Avocados were shown to be more effective than a low-fat diet. A low-fat diet lowered LDL cholesterol levels but also lowered HDL cholesterol, while eating avocados had no effect on HDL cholesterol.

APPLES

The pectin in apples is believed to be responsible for its incredible cholesterol-lowering abilities. Two to three apples a day were added to the diets of middle-aged men and women for 1 month. LDL cholesterol fell more than 10% in half of the participants in the study.

CARROTS

Like apples, carrots also contain an abundance of pectin and other anticholesterol-soluble fibers. Eating a few carrots a day can lower LDL cholesterol by 10 to 20% and raise HDL cholesterol as well. The advantage of eating carrots is that the fiber remains therapeutic whether they are eaten raw, cooked, frozen, canned, chopped or even liquefied.

WATER SOLUBLE FIBERS

Adequate amounts of water-soluble dietary fiber are missing in the diet of the average American. They are critical in any heart disease prevention diet. Studies conducted with these fibers, as well as oat bran and legumes, have all shown significant cholesterol-lowering effects. Water-soluble dietary fiber not only protects directly against heart disease, it also helps to control diabetes, and when added to a weight-loss program can help to control hunger. They are great for losing weight because they add no calories to the diet. In addition, water-soluble dietary fibers are also thought to reduce the risk of colon cancer, alleviate constipation, prevent hemorrhoids, intestinal polyps and diverticulosis. The best sources of this important type of fiber are:

psyllium husk	legumes
pectin	butter beans
guar gum	baked beans
locust bean gum	black beans
acacia	navy beans
	chickpeas

PSYLLIUM

Psyllium seed husk, which is a form of fiber, has been shown to lower heart disease risks. What is psyllium? Until recently, the only place one might find psyllium is in laxatives where it is a major ingredient. But within the past few years, psyllium has garnered attention from the American Heart Association and the Food and Drug Administration (FDA), who recently deemed that foods containing psyllium could carry a "good-for-your-heart" label. Now, food companies are beginning to include psyllium in cereals and other products that contain fiber. Psyllium is such a thick fiber that some people find it hard to swallow, so it's not for everyone. Four servings of 1. 7 grams each per day have been shown to help reduce cholesterol concentrations in the blood.

FOODS WITH CHOLESTEROL-FIGHTING FIBER

Soluble fiber is a key cholesterol-lowering agent in foods. The more fiber foods contain, the more effective they are in cutting LDL cholesterol levels. Six grams of soluble fiber a day should help to lower cholesterol levels to acceptable ranges and keep them there.

vegetables with fiber	Brussels sprouts parsnips turnips okra peas broccoli onions

fruit with fiber	oranges apricots mangos

GRAPEFRUIT PULP

Studies have shown that the segments, membranes and tiny juice sacs of grapefruit — what we refer to as the pulp — have a unique ability to lower cholesterol levels. They contain a soluble fiber called galacturonic acid that not only helps to lower blood cholesterol, but might also help to dissolve or reverse plaque already clogged in arteries. In one study, researchers found that the grapefruit fiber found in about 2½ cups of grapefruit segments eaten every day lowered blood cholesterol levels by about 10%.

FOODS THAT CONTROL BLOOD CLOTS

Foods that prevent blood from clotting also help in the prevention of heart attacks. This ability in some foods is viewed as just as important as the ability in other foods to lower cholesterol levels. Since blood clots are what finally block arteries completely during a heart attack, foods that prevent the blood from clotting and thickening can also help avoid a heart attack. Diet can have an enormous influence on how the blood flows, its viscosity, its stickiness and the tendency for clots to form and enlarge. Foods that prevent blood clots work faster to prevent blood clotting than the foods that work to lower cholesterol levels. Within 1 year, the risk of heart attack can be greatly reduced by sticking with foods that will regulate the blood's clotting ability.

some effective blood clot-fighting foods

garlic and onions

herring, sardines, tuna, mackerel and salmon

red wine

tea

fruits & vegetables high in vitamin C and fiber

hot chile peppers

black mushrooms

olive oil

heart
disease

treatment &
prevention

HEART DISEASE SCREENING & DETECTION

WITH HEART DISEASE as the number 1 killer in the United States, its detection is a main priority for doctors and patients. Since it takes many years for heart disease to develop, most physicians begin to screen early and are conscious of the risks their patients may face even at a young age. The goal is to educate patients as to the risks and motivate them to take action to make the lifestyle and diet modifications vital to prevent the onset of coronary artery disease.

BLOOD CHOLESTEROL SCREENING

SINCE WE KNOW that high cholesterol levels increase the incidence of heart disease, most doctors believe that they can find patients at risk by finding those with high cholesterol levels. Blood cholesterol screening is commonly used to measure the amount of cholesterol in one's blood. Experts agree that having your cholesterol measured is one of the cheapest, most reliable ways to determine your risk of heart disease. Most patients will be instructed to modify their diets and to exercise if cholesterol levels are moderately above the normal range. For others, physicians may suggest losing weight as well.

STRESS TESTING

STRESS TESTING is done frequently to determine the risk of heart disease. It is also used on patients who have already been diagnosed with coronary heart disease so that doctors can estimate the severity of the blockages. In addition, it is used after heart surgery to help doctors monitor the success of the procedure as well as determine an appropriate rehabilitation program.

With a stress test, the patient performs a simple exercise, usually on a treadmill, while his body is monitored using several different devices. These devices may include an electrocardiograph (ECG) machine, an ultrasound machine, a blood pressure cuff and a mask. The ECG records the heart's electrical activity through electrodes that are taped to the back and chest. An ultrasound machine also monitors the heart's activity. The blood pressure cuff constantly monitors the blood pressure and the mask may be used periodically throughout the test to measure oxygen use.

During the 10-minute test, the doctor gradually increases the speed of the treadmill every 2 to 3 minutes while monitoring the heart's performance. The doctor is able to closely observe the heart's function and the oxygen flow in response to increased difficulty. Changes in the ECG pattern or blood pressure and/or unusual shortness of breath may indicate coronary heart disease. If the test indicates blockages, then more tests are usually performed to confirm the diagnosis.

If the test is successful and the patient did not have an abnormal ECG or unusual blood pressure variations, it is likely that the risk of coronary heart disease is low. Stress tests are able to detect individuals with heart disease nearly 90% of the time.

ANGINA

A CONDITION KNOWN AS ANGINA helps physicians determine if heart disease is present. When artherosclerosis is detected before a heart attack occurs, it often manifests itself in the form of angina. Angina is severe chest pain, which occurs when the fatty plaques on the artery walls tear or break apart and allow blood platelets to collect in the opening. This collection of blood platelets causes a blood clot and more cells attach themselves to the clot. The clot then obstructs blood flow to the heart, which in turn deprives the heart of oxygen and causes chest pain or angina.

HEART DISEASE
treatment methods

WHEN HEART DISEASE IS DETECTED EARLY, treatment centers on lowering the amount of cholesterol in one's bloodstream, which unclogs the arteries and restores healthy blood flow. This is most easily accomplished by making changes in diet and lifestyle. In more severe cases, where cholesterol levels are dangerously high, or a heart attack has already occurred, physicians resort to treatment with cholesterol-lowering drugs or surgery.

CONVENTIONAL DRUG THERAPY

DUE TO AGGRESSIVE MARKETING by drug companies, cholesterol-lowering drugs are prescribed to Americans at an astounding rate. Approximately 30 million prescriptions are written each year for these types of drugs. Yet, many of them have not been on the market long enough to understand their long-term effects. And even though they do lower one's cholesterol levels and reduce the risk of heart attack, they also have been shown to increase the mortality rate from other causes. This has occurred because most of these drugs are toxic to the liver and maybe carcinogenic. Even though cholesterol-lowering drugs are widely used, they should only be viewed as a last resort for patients at high risk for heart attack or stroke.

INVASIVE HEART DISEASE TREATMENTS

THE TWO MOST COMMONLY used invasive treatment techniques for heart disease are coronary bypass surgery and balloon angioplasty. These procedures are used to clear blockages in the arteries so that an adequate amount of blood is able to reach the heart. As we already know, heart disease is hard to detect often until a heart attack occurs. Some patients have severe angina, which reveals the presence of heart disease and the need in some cases for surgery. With both treatments, angina is significantly decreased, if not eliminated, and the patient's blood is able to reach the heart more easily.

CORONARY BYPASS SURGERY

WHEN ONE OR MORE coronary arteries are blocked by plaque, causing a decrease in the heart's supply of blood and oxygen, doctors often decide to perform coronary bypass surgery. During surgery, a new channel is created around the blocked artery so that blood can continue to flow to the heart. Blood vessels from the patient's own body are taken from either a leg vein or a mammary artery so that they can be grafted both above and below the blockage. When the grafts are attached successfully, the patient has a new, clear and improved path for blood to flow to the heart. The new path effectively bypasses the blocked area.

Bypass surgery has been performed for more than 25 years. In fact, more than 250,000 bypass procedures are performed in the United States each year, making it the most frequently performed major surgery in the United States. Some patients undergo double, triple or even quadruple bypass operations, depending on how much of their arteries need to be repaired. In the past few years, bypass surgery has become much safer than it used to be. Today it is considered to be 95 to 98% successful, meaning that between 2 and 5% of all patients have complications, including death.

The main risk of bypass surgery is infection and heavy bleeding. Sometimes emergency bypass surgery is performed when a patient enters the hospital with a heart attack and his arteries are severely blocked.

BALLOON ANGIOPLASTY

BALLOON ANGIOPLASTY (percutaneous transluminal coronary angioplasty) or PTCA is an invasive procedure designed to dilate narrowed coronary arteries that are restricting blood flow to the heart and if left untreated could lead to a heart attack. Approximately 400,000 patients undergo this treatment each year. The procedure creates a space in the blocked artery by inserting and then inflating a tiny balloon, which compresses some of the plaque on the walls of the artery. When the balloon is deflated and removed, the plaque remains pressed against the side of the artery, so that space is cleared for improved blood flow. Angioplasty may not always clear an artery completely, depending on where the blockage is. However, 90% of all procedures are successful.

Since angioplasty is less invasive than bypass surgery, it is less risky and the recovery period is faster. Angioplasty was first performed in the late '70s and it is considered the treatment of choice for some heart disease patients. Approximately $\frac{1}{3}$ to $\frac{1}{2}$ of all blockages return and the artery narrows again. This might happen within 6 months of having the procedure. Despite this drawback, studies have shown nearly identical survival rates of over 5 years for both angioplasty and bypass patients.

The main risk associated with angioplasty is the possibility that the artery will collapse immediately during surgery. This will trigger a heart attack and doctors would need to perform emergency bypass surgery immediately. This occurs in 3 to 5% of the cases.

HEART DISEASE PREVENTION TIPS

IT CANNOT BE EMPHASIZED more strongly that reducing heart disease risk should be of paramount concern for most Americans. In the U.S. each year, approximately 800,000 previously healthy persons have their first heart attack, and at least $\frac{1}{4}$ of these people die as a result. Therefore, if one waits until a heart attack strikes, it's too late. Prevention should be woven into one's everyday lifestyle so that a fatal heart attack never has the chance to strike.

For most people, lifestyle modifications of diet, exercise and weight loss can make all the difference, however, depending on the individual, medications are sometimes needed.

ELIMINATING RISKS OF HEART DISEASE

exercise and eat right   atherosclerosis can be stopped and even reversed through proper dietary and lifestyle habits.

stop smoking   smoking and cigarette smoke, even if it's secondhand, is harmful for the heart and circulation.

stop worrying   stress and worrying have proven to be factors linked to heart disease and hypertension.

JUST AS THERE ARE many factors that contribute to heart disease, there are also many strategies one can employ to reduce risk. The following strategies are proven to lower the risk of heart disease for people who do not yet have atherosclerosis as well as for those who already suffer from it.

- exercise
- stress reduction
- weight loss
- controlling diabetes
- controlling high blood pressure

- smoking cessation
- taking aspirin
- estrogen replacement therapy for post-menopausal women
- cholesterol reduction

Increase amount of physical activity and exercise regularly 3 to 4 times per week for 30 minutes.

EXERCISE

LACK OF EXERCISE HAS BEEN identified as an important predictor of death from cardiovascular disease. Being unfit carries with it about the same risk of dying of heart disease as a high cholesterol reading. Conversely, moderate and high levels of fitness have shown to protect against other risk factors. Even though multiple risks increase the odds for death, those who are fit with multiple risk factors are less likely to die of heart disease than those who are out of shape with no other risk factors.

Why is exercise so good for the heart? Physical activity results in calories burned, which leads to weight loss. With this weight loss, the body gleans many additional benefits, including a decrease in blood pressure and cholesterol levels and a lowered risk of diabetes. By improving these 3 major risk factors for cardiovascular disease, exercise greatly reduces the risk that cholesterol will cause blockages in the arteries or that atherosclerosis will develop. Exercise is also beneficial because it prepares the heart and blood vessels for high-stress situations. The heart becomes used to performing at an increased level, as it does during exercise, making it better able to react more efficiently in an emergency. Regular physical activity results in more effective dilation of the blood vessels, which improves overall blood flow. When blood vessels do not dilate regularly, they respond much more slowly when called into action.

Exercise also provides an emotional benefit by raising endorphin levels, which boost one's feeling of well-being. Since stress has been identified as a heart disease risk factor, exercise's ability to improve one's sense of well-being is also an important reason to maintain a regular exercise routine.

exercise reduces the risk of heart disease by

lowering cholesterol levels

increasing the supply of oxygen and blood to the heart

augmenting the functional capacity of the heart

reducing blood pressure

reducing obesity

improving blood clotting mechanisms

Learn to handle stress in healthy ways. Practice stress management and/or reduction techniques, such as meditation, yoga or an exercise program.

STRESS REDUCTION

HIGH STRESS AND ATHEROSCLEROSIS have been linked in several studies. It is believed that the body's reaction to stress may contribute to the progression and the development of heart disease. Some individuals who experience extreme reactions to mental stress have been shown to be more prone to developing artherosclerosis. High stress raises blood pressure and it is believed that when this occurs frequently or in severe cases, damage to the inner linings of blood vessels can result.

stress facts

abnormalities in heart rhythm, due to stress, are more likely to occur on Mondays and Fridays

morning is the most stressful time of the day

overtime and long commutes increase cardiovascular risk

stressed-out working moms are at greater risk than working women without children

Achieve and maintain desirable weight.

WEIGHT LOSS

BECAUSE OBESITY CAN lead to diabetes, and diabetes is a major risk factor for heart disease, being overweight fosters the progression of heart disease. Individuals who are overweight often overlook this connection between diabetes and heart disease. In order to lower risks, doctors recommend that obese people lose their excess pounds to improve heart disease risk. Losing weight can also decrease high cholesterol and high blood pressure.

Limit consumption to a daily maximum of 2 drinks.

LIMIT CONSUMPTION OF ALCOHOL

STUDIES HAVE SHOWN that 2 drinks a day can significantly lower your chances of developing heart disease. Men who averaged ½ to 1 drink a day had 21% less coronary artery disease than abstainers. Those who drank 1 to 2 drinks a day were able to reduce their chances of heart disease by 32%. Because heavier drinking can bring on other dangerous illnesses, the acceptable and safe limit for heart disease prevention is 2 drinks a day. Researchers believe that alcohol is beneficial because it raises levels of HDL cholesterol and red wine in particular is an anticoagulant. Alcoholic beverages also contain antioxidants.

Should a nondrinker start to drink to reduce the risk of heart disease? This question is frequently posed to physicians and the answer is, no. Although alcohol does reduce heart disease risk, there are other more powerful ways to reduce it than to take up drinking. But for those who already drink, if they can limit their consumption to 2 drinks a day it should help to decrease heart disease risk.

First be tested and then if afflicted, control the condition as vigorously as possible.

CONTROLLING DIABETES

WE ALREADY KNOW that diabetes is a major risk factor for heart disease, so controlling it will help to prevent its onset. The first step in controlling diabetes effectively is to be tested periodically to find out if you have it. The American Diabetic Association recommends testing every 3 years for all adults over the age of 45. Testing is vitally important for individuals in high-risk groups, such as those who are obese, African Americans, Hispanics and American Indians, or those that have a close relative with diabetes. With early diagnosis and treatment comes better prevention against heart disease. If diabetes has not progressed to its advanced stages, where it can cause irreversible harm to the body, it can be treated with diet modifications, weight loss and exercise. Medications are used in cases where lifestyle modifications are not adequate enough to control the illness.

140/90 mm hg or less

CONTROLLING HIGH BLOOD PRESSURE

HIGH BLOOD PRESSURE can be reduced in most people by diet and lifestyle modifications. It is known that salt intake can increase blood pressure, so sticking to a low-salt diet is key to restoring blood pressure to safe levels. In addition, high blood pressure is often caused by excessive alcohol consumption and controlling this factor can help to reduce blood pressure. Patients who are able to stop smoking, exercise more and eat a healthier diet are able to significantly lower their blood pressure and reduce their risk for heart attack.

Complete cessation.

SMOKING CESSATION

DESPITE THE AGGRESSIVE public health campaign and years of publicity about the dangers of smoking, ¼ of the U.S. population still smokes. Although ⅔ of all smokers say they would like to quit if they could, most are not able to kick the habit. Only 3% of smokers successfully quit each year. Elimination of all smokers in the United States would cut the incidence of heart attacks dramatically. If the U.S. were a smoke-free society, this factor alone would reduce heart attack rates more than any other factor. Studies have shown that smoking raises the risk of heart attack even more in women than it does in men. Women who smoke are 50% more likely to suffer from a heart attack than men who smoke.

Researchers are working hard to find medications and strategies to help smokers overcome their addiction. Currently, there are several prescription drugs available aimed at overcoming addiction. In addition, there are many over-the-counter smoking cessation products designed to treat nicotine addiction, such as the patch, gum, nasal sprays and inhalers.

tips for quitting smoking	set a quit date within 2 weeks
	ask for support from friends, family and co-workers
	remove all cigarettes from your home, office and car
	review past attempts to quit and why they didn't work
	prepare for challenges within the first few weeks, especially nicotine withdrawal

ASPIRIN & HEART ATTACK PREVENTION

THE AMERICAN HEART ASSOCIATION recently stated that Americans should make greater use of aspirin in their fight against heart attacks. Aspirin is proven to prevent blood clots, which can cause heart attacks and strokes. It is estimated that up to 10,000 more people would survive heart attacks if they took 1 aspirin (325 milligrams) when they had chest pains or other signs of a heart attack. One study showed that heart attack patients who took aspirin immediately after their symptoms began and continued taking aspirin daily for 1 month had a 23% lower risk of dying of heart disease, and almost 50% lower risk of having a stroke, or second heart attack compared to patients who did not take aspirin.

Aspirin, along with other medications that individuals can take to prevent against heart attacks, should not be a substitute for maintaining a healthy lifestyle and exercising. As with all other medications, individuals should consult their physicians before starting a daily aspirin regimen.

ESTROGEN REPLACEMENT THERAPY FOR POST-MENOPAUSAL WOMEN

It is startling to learn that many women do not think they are at risk for heart disease. Despite the fact that heart attack, stroke and other cardiovascular diseases are the leading cause of death among women, only 31% of women in the United States know it. Many women view cancer as their biggest threat and look upon heart disease as an illness that more often strikes men. However, twice as many women die from cardiovascular diseases than from all forms of cancer, even breast cancer. Ten times more women die from cardiovascular diseases than from breast cancer. Indeed, more women die of heart diseases than succumb to all of the next 16 leading causes of death. The American Heart Association recently announced that close to ½ of American women die of cardiovascular disease. Women of all ages who are overweight and have high cholesterol levels are at risk. Women should follow the same strategies for men to lower their risk for heart disease, and some women may even want to consider hormone replacement therapy.

Estrogen replacement therapy for post-menopausal women has been the subject of numerous studies to determine whether it is beneficial. Much controversy surrounds the use of estrogen replacement therapy because of the increased risk of breast cancer associated with it. Nevertheless, studies have shown that estrogen improves coronary risk factor profiles as well as coronary blood flow. Estrogen replacement therapy reduces a woman's risk of heart disease by lowering her bad LDL cholesterol and increasing the good HDL cholesterol. Moreover, experimental evidence reveals that estrogen helps to prevent abnormal blood vessel constriction. Until further research is carried out, physicians only recommend estrogen replacement therapy for women with one or more risk factors for heart disease. They are likely to obtain the greatest benefit from hormone replacement. For women with any of the following risk factors: cigarette smokers, high blood pressure, elevated cholesterol levels or obesity, hormone replacement therapy can help to reduce their risk. If women are not at high risk for heart disease, estrogen replacement therapy would most likely not be a recommended course of therapy. However, a physician must carefully examine each woman's individual profile before she should begin hormone replacement therapy.

LDL cholesterol should be less than 160 mg/dL if no more than 1 risk factor is present, or LDL cholesterol should be less than 130 mg/dL if 2 or more risk factors are present

HDL cholesterol should be greater than 35 mg/dL and triglycerides should be less than 200 mg/dL

CHOLESTEROL MANAGEMENT

SINCE CHOLESTEROL LEVELS in the blood directly impact who develops heart disease, this risk factor should be managed and controlled assiduously. In most cases, cholesterol levels are determined solely by what one eats, so maintaining a healthy diet can keep cholesterol levels in check and reduce the risk of heart disease.

recipes
for a healthy heart

introduction

breakfast

Fruit

Fruit Shakes

Cold Cereals

Cooked Cereals

Muffins & Breads

Pancakes, Coffee Cakes, Eggs & Sides

Breakfast Alternatives

appetizers,
snacks & drinks

Appetizers

Snacks

Drinks

Tea Drinks

Soy Drinks

soups, salads & sides

Salads

Soups

Sides

main dishes

Fish & Seafood

Poultry

Meats

Game

Vegetables

desserts

Cakes

Pies

Puddings

Cookies & Other Treats

a word about
the recipes

ENJOYING A DELICIOUS MEAL with family and friends is one of life's simple pleasures. By using some of today's modern and alternative methods to cooking, you can learn to prepare good-tasting and health-promoting food. Taking the time to nourish oneself in a healthful way is the key to eating well. Learn how to select and prepare foods that promote long-term health for you and your family. The recipes that follow aim to bring not only nourishment, but also dining pleasure.

These recipes feature different ways to prepare foods that promote and maintain a healthy heart. Imagine, finally a way to enjoy "gourmet dining" with low-fat and low-cholesterol alternatives. What could be more delightful than beginning the day with chilled cantaloupe, crusty Tuscano wheat bread, honey-sesame ricotta and a warm, creamy latte? This breakfast provides a rich source of fruit, grains, fiber, seeds, potassium, vitamin C, E and B vitamins and calcium.

By preparing and modifying some key ingredients, you can create great-tasting and healthful dishes. These recipes will teach you how to reduce quantities, substitute ingredients and interchange cooking methods.

If you like the flavor of butter, learn how to use it sparingly and still achieve the proper taste. Reduce the need for fattening shortening ingredients by substituting fruit purees. Use herbs, spices, marinades, vinegars, mustards, chutneys and salsas to intensify flavors. Try oven roasting and broiling instead of deep-frying, or microwave cooking in place of sautéing. These dishes will add great taste as well as benefit your heart and overall health.

Most of the following recipes serve 4 to 6 people. Each recipe gives nutritional information on vitamins and other important information.

As with all the other pleasures in life, dining well is dining with ease and moderation. Eat slowly — take the time to enjoy the color, aroma, texture and flavor of the food. Savor the composition of the dessert — and indulge your palate.

BREAKFAST
RECIPES

muffins & breads

- Chewy Flax-Bran Muffins
- Pecan Pie Muffins
- Hazelnut-Fig Muffins
- Buttermilk Berry Muffins
- Cream Cheese Topping
- Tuscano Wheat Bread
- Saltless French Bread
- Oatmeal-Raisin Nut Bread

pancakes, coffee cakes, eggs & sides

- Citrus-Kiwi Buttermilk Pancakes
- Apricot Coffee Cake
- Hearty Breakfast Omelet
- Tri-Color Pepper Fritatta

breakfast alternatives

- Water Bagels
- Prepared Fish

BREAKFAST is the most important meal of the day. How many times have we heard that statement and dismissed it? Breakfast has become a quick coffee and pastry while we're heading out the door. It is time to rethink what we are eating in the morning, and learn to begin the day with a well-balanced breakfast.

The recipes that follow are flavorful and quick and provide vitamins, minerals and the fiber necessary for optimum health. If you suffer from hunger pangs by 10 a.m. or are guilty of eating empty calorie meals, then get ready to feel energized by smoothies and great-tasting muffins. All are portable and can be enjoyed at home or en route to the office.

BREAKFAST IS THE BEST time to begin eating fruit. Many fruits contain vitamins and minerals necessary for cholesterol reduction.

CANTALOUPE WITH LIME SLICES

There's nothing more refreshing than starting the day with a cool slice of cantaloupe.

1 cantaloupe, chilled

1 lime

4 fresh mint sprigs

nutritional analysis per serving

Calories (kcal) 52.2
Total Fat (g) 0.4
Cholesterol (mg) 0
Sodium (mg) 13
Potassium (mg) 432
Vitamin C (mg) 62

MAKES 4 SERVINGS

Wash, peel and cut cantaloupe into 8 slices. Cut lime into 4 wedges. On each of 4 chilled plates, arrange 2 cantaloupe slices. Garnish with lime wedges and mint sprigs.

VARIATION   Substitute other melons such as honeydew, casaba and Crenshaw. Garnish melon with lemon wedges and fresh lemon thyme. Cut chilled papaya in half. Remove pulp and seeds, and reserve 1 teaspoonful seeds to sprinkle over cut half. Serve with lemon wedge and fresh mint.

FRUIT WITH YOGURT AND WHEAT BERRIES

Tangy yogurt is the perfect topping for ripe fresh fruit. Precook the wheat berries in the microwave oven and store them covered in the refrigerator for up to a week. They make chewy additions to most fruit and vegetables.

1 cup hard red winter wheat
   berries, rinsed and drained

3 cups water

1 banana

2 large apricots

2 kiwi fruit

8 strawberries

1 mango

4 cups nonfat plain yogurt

MAKES 8 SERVINGS

nutritional analysis per serving

Calories (kcal)	290.9
Total Fat (g)	1.9
Cholesterol (mg)	2
Sodium (mg)	93
Potassium (mg)	764
Vitamin C (mg)	106

In a 2-quart microwave-safe bowl, cook wheat berries in water on full power until boiling, about 8 minutes. Reduce power to medium, cover and cook until berries are tender and no liquid remains, about 40 minutes. Cool, cover and refrigerate until ready to use.

Alternately, heat wheat berries and water in a medium saucepan on high heat. Bring to a boil, about 5 minutes. Lower heat, cover and simmer until wheat berries are tender and the liquid is absorbed, about 1 hour.

Slice and divide the fruit evenly among 8 small bowls. Top each serving with ½ cup of the yogurt and ¼ cup of the wheat berries.

VARIATIONS   Since fruit varies with the season, there is a wide variety of flavorful combinations. Use summer fruit like berries, stone fruit, melons or grapes. Try apples, pears, figs, persimmons, apples, pears and dried fruit like raisins, apricots, figs and cranberries in the fall and winter seasons. Creativity abounds with selections like these and yogurt complements them all!

Fruit with Yogurt and Wheat Berries

Cooked grains also go well with fruit and yogurt. Try 7- or 10-grain cereal, millet, quinoa, rolled and steel-cut oats and spelt berries. Use sunflower, sesame and flaxseed, toasted wheat germ, dry oat and wheat bran, brewers' yeast, chopped walnuts, hazelnuts, almonds, Brazil nuts, cashews and soy nuts as additional toppings.

NOTE   Yogurt is an acquired taste for some people who object to its tart, somewhat sharp flavor. Sampling various brands of yogurt may be necessary to find one that pleases your palate. Russian and Greek-style yogurts tend to be the mildest tasting.

HONEY-SESAME RICOTTA

Mediterranean influences are evident with this unusual breakfast treat. *Tuscano Wheat Bread*, page 100, contrasts with the creamy softness of the honeyed ricotta.

4 cups nonfat ricotta cheese

8 figs, sliced

8 tablespoons honey

4 tablespoons sesame seeds

4 thick slices whole wheat
   bread, toasted

MAKES 4 SERVINGS

nutritional
analysis
per serving

Calories (kcal)	525.6
Total Fat (g)	10.8
Cholesterol (mg)	19
Sodium (mg)	1057
Potassium (mg)	560
Vitamin C (mg)	2

Divide ricotta among 4 serving dishes. Arrange fig slices around ricotta and drizzle honey over ricotta. Sprinkle with sesame seeds. Serve with wheat bread and additional honey.

WHEN YOU'RE ON THE GO and don't have much time for breakfast, try these nutritious drinks. They can help give you the energy to get you through the morning. To save time, prepare and freeze fruit for the shakes the night before. You may not need to use ice cubes if you're using frozen fruit. Add a chewy, multi-grain muffin and you're ready to start the day!

STRAWBERRY, BANANA AND KIWI SMOOTHIE
Fill your glass with sweet strawberries, mellow bananas and tart kiwi for a creamy smoothie.

1 cup vanilla-flavored soy milk
½ cup sliced strawberries
½ kiwi, sliced
½ banana, sliced

nutritional analysis per serving

Calories (kcal) 202.6
Total Fat (g) 5.6
Cholesterol (mg) 0
Sodium (mg) 35
Potassium (mg) 849
Vitamin C (mg) 77
Vitamin E

MAKES 2 SERVINGS

Pour soy milk into a blender container. Remove stems from strawberries and remove skin from kiwi. Add fruit. Blend on low speed to chop and finish on high speed to blend. When thick and creamy, pour into a frosty glass or chilled travel mug.

APRICOT, MANGO AND LIME COOLER

Yogurt and lime juice add a pleasant tang to this tropical cooler.

½ cup nonfat plain yogurt
2 tablespoons honey
juice of 1 lime
½ cup sliced apricots
½ mango, cubed
7 ice cubes

MAKES 2 SERVINGS

nutritional
analysis
per serving

Calories (kcal)	181.3
Total Fat (g)	0.5
Cholesterol (mg)	1
Sodium (mg)	49
Potassium (mg)	484
Vitamin C (mg)	55

Pour yogurt, honey and lime juice into a blender container. Remove core from apricots. Remove skin and slice fruit from pit of mango. Add fruit. Blend on low speed to chop and finish on high speed to blend. When thick and creamy, pour into a frosty glass or chilled travel mug.

NOTE   Mangoes can be cubed easily by first cutting 3 slices around the pit to loosen and remove the pit. With each slice, score the flesh of the fruit down to, but not through the thick skin. Hold a prepared slice in each hand, and with your thumb, gently push on the skin so the flesh pops up. Remove the cubes by running a sharp knife under the fruit above the skin.

MINTED CANTALOUPE FRAPPÉ

Using frozen fruit produces a thicker and cooler smoothie.

½ cup silken tofu*

2 tablespoons frozen apple
   juice concentrate

1 cup frozen cantaloupe
   chunks

2 tablespoons finely chopped
   fresh mint leaves

MAKES 1 SERVING

nutritional analysis per serving	
Calories (kcal)	202.6
Total Fat (g)	5.6
Cholesterol (mg)	0
Sodium (mg)	35
Potassium (mg)	849
Vitamin C (mg)	77
Vitamin E	

Pour tofu and apple juice into a blender container. Add cantaloupe chunks. Blend on low speed to chop and finish on high speed to blend. When thick and creamy, pour into a frosty glass or chilled travel mug.

* See NOTE on page 104 for more information on where to purchase silken tofu.

SPICY FRUIT SHAKE

Pour this shake into a tall glass and refresh yourself on a warm summer day.

½ cup nonfat milk

2 tablespoons frozen orange
    juice concentrate

¼ cup instant powdered
    nonfat milk

½ papaya, sliced

1 banana, sliced

¼ teaspoon ground ginger

½ teaspoon cinnamon

¼ teaspoon nutmeg

MAKES 2 SERVINGS

nutritional analysis per serving	
Calories (kcal)	193.6
Total Fat (g)	4.9
Cholesterol (mg)	17
Sodium (mg)	94
Potassium (mg)	772
Vitamin C (mg)	60

Pour milk, orange juice and powdered milk into a blender container. Remove skin and seeds from papaya. Add fruit and spices. Blend on low speed to chop and finish on high speed to blend. When thick and creamy, pour into a frosty glass or chilled travel mug.

Because of the avid interest in health and nutrition, many food suppliers are making an effort to offer cereals with grains and nuts that are healthful and easy to prepare. Some brands are wholesome and flavorful, while others claiming to be healthful have ingredients high in fat and sodium. To make sure you're getting the most out of your cereal, try these home-prepared granola and muesli recipes that are easy to make and stay fresh in the refrigerator for several weeks.

Almond-Apricot Granola

This nutty, crunchy granola can be eaten with milk as a cereal, used as a topping for yogurt, added to cookie recipes or enjoyed as a snack. Store in the refrigerator to maintain freshness.

2 cups old-fashioned rolled oats
1 cup oat bran
1 cup wheat germ
¼ cup brewer's yeast
¼ cup flax meal
¼ cup lecithin granules
½ cup sunflower seeds
¼ cup sesame seeds
1½ cups coarsely chopped almonds
¾ cup honey
1 tablespoon almond extract
1 cup slivered dried apricots
¾ cup raisins
fat-free cooking spray

MAKES 8 SERVINGS

nutritional analysis per serving

Calories (kcal) 645.1
Total Fat (g) 31.9
Cholesterol (mg) 0
Sodium (mg) 15
Potassium (mg) 954
Vitamin C (mg) 1
High in Vitamin E

Preheat oven to 300°. In a large stockpot, combine oats, oat bran, wheat germ, brewer's yeast, flax meal, lecithin granules, sunflower seeds, sesame seeds and almonds. Mix well.

In a separate bowl, combine honey and almond extract. Stir well to blend. Drizzle over dry ingredients and toss gently. Spray an 11 x 15 baking sheet with fat-free cooking spray and spread granola mixture evenly with a rubber spatula. Place sheet in middle of oven.

Bake until crisp and toasted, about 40 to 50 minutes, stirring every 10 minutes. Remove from oven. Cool, and stir in apricots and raisins. Lightly pack into glass jars and refrigerate.

PEANUT-OAT MUESLI

Peanut butter fans will enjoy beginning the day with a serving of this quick and easy breakfast in a bowl.

1 cup quick-cooking oats

½ cup oat bran

½ cup wheat germ

¾ cup unsalted dry-roasted peanuts

½ cup sunflower seeds

2 bananas, sliced

1 unpeeled apple, chopped

2 tablespoons honey

cold nonfat milk, soy milk, or nonfat plain yogurt

MAKES 4 SERVINGS

nutritional analysis per serving

Calories (kcal) 519.5
Total Fat (g) 26.3
Cholesterol (mg) 0
Sodium (mg) 210
Potassium (mg) 832
Vitamin C (mg) 7
High in Vitamin E

In a large bowl, combine oats, oat bran, wheat germ, roasted peanuts and sunflower seeds. Divide among 4 cereal bowls. Top each serving with bananas, apples and honey. Pour in milk or top with yogurt.

NOTE   Muesli means "mixture" in German. It can include raw or toasted grains, dried fruit and dried milk solids. It's usually eaten with milk, yogurt or fruit juice. Developed by a Swiss nutritionist near the end of the nineteenth century, it is the forerunner of today's granola.

Modern Day Muesli

Keeping with the current trend of intensifying flavor with herbs and spices, try adding cardamom, cinnamon and allspice to your next basic muesli mixture. Bottled mango nectar gives a nice finishing touch to the mixture.

1 cup quick-cooking oats

½ cup wheat bran

½ cup wheat germ

1 teaspoon dry-roasted soy nuts

1 tablespoon flaxseeds

1 tablespoon sunflower seeds

½ cup chopped dried mango slices

½ teaspoon cardamom

½ teaspoon cinnamon

¼ teaspoon allspice

1 can (11.5 fluid ounces) mango nectar

nutritional analysis per serving	
Calories (kcal) 197.2
Total Fat (g) 4.2
Cholesterol (mg) 0
Sodium (mg) 215
Potassium (mg) 339
Vitamin C (mg) 28
High in Vitamin E

In a large bowl, mix together oats, bran, wheat germ, soy nuts, flaxseeds, sunflower seeds and mango slices. Sprinkle mixture with cardamom, cinnamon and allspice. Mix well. Divide among 4 bowls and serve with mango nectar.

VARIATION Use chocolate-flavored soy milk or nonfat chocolate milk instead of mango nectar. Substitute fresh strawberry or raspberry slices for the dried mango.

MAKES 4 SERVINGS

THE WIDE SELECTION OF whole grains available today allows us to create a variety of wholesome, delicious meals easily and economically. Beginning the day with cooked cereal nourishes, energizes and satisfies the appetite well into the lunch hour.

Always rinse grains thoroughly in running cold water, and strain to remove any grit or debris. All grains can be cooked on the stovetop. Soaking grains overnight in cold water or cooking in a microwave shortens the cooking time.

Seven-Grain Cereal

Perhaps the easiest to prepare and the most interesting to eat, this cereal offers the flavor of wheat, oats, wheat bran, soybeans, barley, corn and millet. Nonfat yogurt, dried and fresh fruit combined with sunflower seeds and dry-roasted peanuts will add a flavorful bang to your day. Whet the appetite with a fresh grapefruit and a nonfat latte.

1 cup 7-grain cereal
2¼ cups cold water
2 cups nonfat plain yogurt
1 cup sliced dried figs
2 bananas, sliced
2 cups sliced strawberries
½ cup sunflower seeds
½ cup unsalted dry-roasted
    peanuts

Makes 4 servings

nutritional
analysis
per serving

Calories (kcal) 551.7
Total Fat (g) 21.2
Cholesterol (mg) 2
Sodium (mg) 101
Potassium (mg) 1329
Vitamin C (mg) 7
Vitamin E

In a medium saucepan, bring water to a boil. Slowly add cereal, stirring constantly until mixed with water. Lower heat. Cover and simmer for 15 minutes. Remove from heat and divide among 4 cereal bowls. Divide and arrange yogurt and fruit around cereal. Top each serving with a portion of sunflower seeds and peanuts. Serve immediately.

DOUBLE-YUM OATMEAL

Steel-cut oats team up with oat bran, Brazil nuts and kiwi fruit for a powerhouse breakfast. Pour warm soy milk sweetened with molasses for extra flavor and nutritional benefits. Steel-cut oats are whole groats that have been steamed and finely cut producing a delightful chewy texture when cooked. To save time in the morning, cook the oats the night before and reheat in the microwave.

1 cup rinsed drained steel-cut
   oats
4½ cups cold water
2 tablespoons molasses
1½ cups soy milk
½ cup oat bran
4 Brazil nuts, chopped
2 kiwi fruit, peeled and cubed

MAKES 6 SERVINGS

nutritional analysis per serving

Calories (kcal) 738.8
Total Fat (g) 64.5
Cholesterol (mg) 0
Sodium (mg) 19
Potassium (mg) 925
Vitamin C (mg) 25
Vitamin E

In a medium saucepan, combine steel-cut oats and cold water. Bring to a boil, cover, lower heat and simmer for 30 to 40 minutes, or until most of the liquid is absorbed. In a small saucepan, combine molasses and soy milk. Heat gently for 5 minutes, or until warm. Remove from heat and set aside. When oats are cooked, remove pan from heat and stir in oat bran, Brazil nuts and kiwi. Divide among 6 heated bowls and serve with warm soy milk mixture.

NOTE Oat bran should be eaten daily to benefit from its cholesterol-fighting properties. It makes a slightly textured, nut-like topping for many foods. Place some in a pretty sugar bowl and offer as a condiment at mealtime. Keep refrigerated when not being used.

Apple and Spice Bulgur Wheat Groats

Bulgur wheat has long been a staple food in the Middle East because of its versatility. It can be served as a hot cereal, a pilaf, stuffing for meats and vegetables, and cold as a filling for pita breads and as a grain in salads. Be sure to buy quick-cooking bulgur. Add chopped apples, raisins and spices for a fast, hot breakfast.

1 cup quick-cooking bulgur

1 cup cold water

1 cup unfiltered apple juice

1 medium unpeeled apple, finely chopped

¼ cup chopped dried prunes

¼ cup chopped dried apricots

1 teaspoon cinnamon

½ teaspoon nutmeg

⅛ teaspoon ground ginger

¼ cup oat bran

¼ cup raisins

¼ cup coarsely chopped cashew nuts

1½ cups warm vanilla-flavored soy milk

Makes 4 servings

nutritional analysis per serving	
Calories (kcal)	290.5
Total Fat (g)	7.8
Cholesterol (mg)	0
Sodium (mg)	223
Potassium (mg)	651
Vitamin C (mg)	4
Vitamin E	

In a medium saucepan, combine bulgur, water and apple juice, and bring to a boil. Lower heat, cover and simmer for 20 minutes, or until most of the liquid is absorbed. Stir in apples, prunes, apricots, cinnamon, nutmeg, ginger and oat bran. Cover, remove from heat source and set aside for 10 minutes. Add raisins and cashews and serve with soy milk.

SUMMER BERRY BREAKFAST
The combination of farina, berries and yogurt is guaranteed to please the "breakfast fussies" in your family, while keeping them healthy, trim and fit. Farina can be purchased in Middle Eastern markets, or use packaged Cream of Wheat cereals.

4 cups water
½ teaspoon salt
¾ cup farina
½ cup brown sugar, packed
1 cup oat bran
3 cups mixed fresh berries
1 cup chopped toasted
   almonds
2 cups nonfat plain yogurt
additional brown sugar

MAKES 4 SERVINGS

nutritional
analysis
per serving

Calories (kcal) 560.7
Total Fat (g) 20.9
Cholesterol (mg) 2
Sodium (mg) 375
Potassium (mg) 983
Vitamin C (mg) 61

In a small saucepan, bring water to a boil. Gradually add salt and farina, stirring constantly. Cover and simmer for 5 minutes. If using wheat cereal, cook for 1 minute. Remove from heat. Cover and set aside until thickened. While still warm, pour into a 1-quart shallow casserole dish. Mix brown sugar with oat bran in a separate bowl and sprinkle evenly over farina. Arrange berries over brown sugar and top with toasted almonds. Serve at room temperature with yogurt and additional brown sugar.

MUFFINS OFFER VITAMINS, minerals, fiber and a little fat combined with grains, seeds, nuts, fruit, vegetables and some dairy. In 30 minutes, you can have a week's supply to enjoy. Home-baked muffins do not contain preservatives, but you can freeze them and reheat as needed.

There is also a wonderful variety of whole grain breads like pumpernickel, rye, oatmeal, whole wheat, flatbread, sourdough, whole wheat pita, corn tortillas, bagels and English muffins. Since many of these are available in the bakery section of food markets, We've included recipes for special breads. The recipes have little or no salt, are low-fat and easy to bake at home. Using a bread machine saves time and is virtually foolproof. Enjoy these breads at mealtime or oven-toasted as snacks.

CHEWY FLAX-BRAN MUFFINS
Muffins are rich in nutrients and make a marvelous breakfast food.

fat-free cooking spray

1 cup flaxseed meal

1 cup oat bran

1 cup all-purpose flour

2½ teaspoons baking powder

1 teaspoon baking soda

1 teaspoon cinnamon

¼ teaspoon ground ginger

½ teaspoon ground cloves

½ cup chopped dried apricots

1 cup chopped walnuts

½ cup low-fat buttermilk

½ cup honey

¼ cup light corn syrup

2 cups peeled, shredded
   carrots, about 3 to 4

¼ cup nonfat plain yogurt

nutritional analysis per serving (1 muffin)

Calories (kcal)	247.1
Total Fat (g)	7.1
Cholesterol (mg)	0
Sodium (mg)	213
Potassium (mg)	344
Vitamin C (mg)	2
Vitamin E	

Preheat oven to 350º. Spray 12 muffin cups with fat-free cooking spray. Combine flaxseed meal, oat bran, flour, baking powder, baking soda, cinnamon, ginger, cloves, apricots and walnuts. Set aside. In a separate bowl, combine buttermilk, honey and corn syrup. Mix well. Fold in carrots and yogurt. Pour buttermilk mixture into flaxseed combination. Stir lightly with a fork, until ingredients are moistened. Fill muffin cups ⅔ full. Bake until tops are golden, but not brown, about 25 to 30 minutes.

MAKES 12 MUFFINS

PECAN PIE MUFFINS

Pecan pie fanciers will enjoy these taste-alike muffins. Pecan oil is available at specialty food markets.

fat-free cooking spray
1 cup whole wheat flour
1 cup oat bran
3 teaspoons baking powder
½ cup plus 2 tablespoons
   coarsely chopped pecans
2 egg whites
2 tablespoons pecan oil
⅓ cup nonfat milk
¾ cup maple syrup
2 teaspoons vanilla extract

MAKES 12 SMALL MUFFINS

nutritional
analysis
per serving
(1 muffin)

Calories (kcal) 170.7
Total Fat (g) 6.9
Cholesterol (mg) 0
Sodium (mg) 106
Potassium (mg) 171
Vitamin C (mg) 0

Preheat oven to 375°. Spray 12 muffin cups with fat-free cooking spray. Combine whole wheat flour, oat bran, baking powder and ½ cup of the pecans. Mix well and set aside. In a separate bowl, whisk together egg whites, pecan oil, nonfat milk, maple syrup and vanilla extract. Pour over dry ingredients. Fold gently with a spatula until mixture is just moistened. Fill muffin cups ⅔ full. Top with remaining 2 tablespoons pecans. Bake until tops are a pale gold color, about 16 minutes.

HAZELNUT-FIG MUFFINS
The Italian touch is evident in these fragrant muffins. The flavors of fig, hazelnut and sweet anise transport one to the sunny Ligurian coast. For a special treat, serve with fresh nonfat ricotta cheese and lavender honey.

fat-free cooking spray

1 cup Grape Nuts

1 cup nonfat milk

1 cup hazelnuts

1¼ cups all-purpose flour

1 tablespoon baking powder

2 teaspoons anise seeds

1 egg white

1 tablespoon nonfat plain
   yogurt

1 cup fig puree

½ cup brown sugar, packed

2 tablespoons hazelnut oil

1 teaspoon anise extract

MAKES 12 MUFFINS

nutritional analysis per serving (1 muffin)	
Calories (kcal)	207.9
Total Fat (g)	86
Cholesterol (mg)	0
Sodium (mg)	176
Potassium (mg)	194
Vitamin C (mg)	1
Vitamin E	

Preheat oven to 400°. Spray 12 muffin cups with fat-free cooking spray. Combine Grape Nuts and milk. Stir and set aside for 10 minutes. Cereal will absorb some of the liquid and soften. On a foil-lined baking sheet, spread hazelnuts evenly. Bake until toasted, about 7 to 10 minutes. Cool, chop and reserve. Turn oven down to 375°. Combine flour, baking powder, anise seeds and hazelnuts. Set aside. When cereal has softened, whisk in egg white, yogurt, fig puree, brown sugar, hazelnut oil and anise extract. Spoon flour mixture over wet ingredients. Using a spatula, gently fold until moistened. Fill muffin cups ⅔ full. Bake until tops are golden brown, about 20 minutes.

VARIATION   Apricot and peach puree may be substituted for fig puree. Use toasted almonds and almond oil in place of hazelnuts and hazelnut oil. Replace anise extract and seeds with 1½ teaspoons almond extract.

NOTE   For a fast and easy way to prepare fruit puree, use 8 ounces of baby food fruit.

BUTTERMILK BERRY MUFFINS

Don't wait for summertime to whip up a batch of these multi-berry muffins. Frozen berries like strawberries, raspberries, blackberries and blueberries are available year-round.

fat-free cooking spray
1 cup whole wheat flour
1¼ cups oat bran
2 teaspoons baking powder
1 teaspoon baking soda
¾ cup brown sugar, packed
2 teaspoons cinnamon
½ cup low-fat buttermilk
¾ cup pureed mixed berries
1 egg white
1 teaspoon almond extract
2 tablespoons canola oil
1 cup sliced mixed berries

MAKES 12 MUFFINS

nutritional analysis per serving (1 muffin)	
Calories (kcal)	128.2
Total Fat (g)	3.4
Cholesterol (mg)	0
Sodium (mg)	185
Potassium (mg)	188
Vitamin C (mg)	12

Preheat oven to 425°. Spray 12 muffin cups with fat-free cooking spray. Combine flour, oat bran, baking powder, baking soda, ½ cup of the brown sugar and 1 teaspoon of the cinnamon. Mix well and set aside. In a separate bowl, whisk together buttermilk, berry puree, egg white, almond extract and canola oil. Fold in ¾ cup of the sliced berries. Spoon buttermilk-berry mixture into dry ingredients. Gently fold until moistened. Fill muffin cups ⅔ full. Place a few of the remaining sliced berries on each muffin. Mix remaining 1 teaspoon of the cinnamon with remaining ¼ cup of the brown sugar. Sprinkle evenly over fruit-topped muffins. Bake until golden brown, about 17 to 20 minutes.

CREAM CHEESE TOPPING
In addition to spreadable fruit, low-fat creamy toppings enhance the flavor of muffins and quick breads.

2 tablespoons orange juice

1 tablespoon grated orange
    zest

3 tablespoons fat-free cream
    cheese

¼ cup plus 2 tablespoons
    confectioners' sugar

nutritional
analysis
per serving
(2 tablespoons)

Calories (kcal) 71.8
Total Fat (g) 1.9
Cholesterol (mg) 6
Sodium (mg) 32
Potassium (mg) 37
Vitamin C (mg) 6

With a blender, whip together orange juice, zest, cream cheese and powdered sugar until smooth and creamy. Use as a topping for baked goods.

MAKES ½ CUP

TUSCANO WHEAT BREAD

Tuscan bread is never baked with salt. This practice dates back to the Middle Ages when an unfair tax was levied on salt. Rather than pay, the proud Tuscans baked saltless bread. This tradition continues today. In this recipe, unfiltered honey becomes the preservative.

2½ teaspoons yeast
1¼ cups warm water
¼ cup honey
4 teaspoons vital wheat gluten
¼ cup all-purpose flour
3¾ cups whole wheat flour
fat-free cooking spray

MAKES 1 (2-POUND) LOAF

nutritional analysis per serving (1-inch slice)

Calories (kcal)	82.3
Total Fat (g)	0.4
Cholesterol (mg)	0
Sodium (mg)	2
Potassium (mg)	88

BREAD MACHINE METHOD In the baking pan of a bread machine, place water, honey, gluten, flours and yeast. Bake according to manufacturer's instructions.

CONVENTIONAL METHOD About 30 minutes before baking, place a baking stone on the center rack of a cold oven. Heat oven to 450°. In a large bowl, stir yeast into ¼ cup of the warm water. When mixture becomes creamy, in about 10 minutes, add remaining 1 cup of water and honey. Mix well. Combine gluten and flours. Gradually beat flour mixture into yeast mixture until thoroughly blended. Turn dough onto a floured surface and knead until firm and elastic, 8 to 10 minutes. Place dough in a bowl lightly sprayed with fat-free cooking spray. Cover tightly with plastic wrap. When doubled, in about 1 to 1½ hours, turn dough out onto a floured surface. Flatten slightly, shape into one large oval and place on a cornmeal-dusted baking sheet. Dust the top lightly with flour, cover with a slightly damp towel and let rise until doubled, about 45 to 60 minutes. Place baking sheet on stone and bake for 15 minutes. Reduce heat to 400°. Bake until bread is golden and sounds hollow when tapped, about 30 to 35 minutes. Remove and cool on wire racks.

NOTE Use nonstick cooking utensils. Place dough in a nonstick, 8 quart-wide pot rather than a ceramic bowl to lessen sticking.

SALTLESS FRENCH BREAD

This crusty French bread is a good base for fruit spreads, nut butters or unfiltered honey, topped with toasted wheat germ or oat bran. The yogurt boosts the calcium content.

2½ teaspoons yeast
½ cup warm water
½ cup nonfat milk
½ cup nonfat plain yogurt
3 teaspoons vital wheat gluten
3 cups all-purpose flour
fat-free cooking spray

MAKES 1 (2-POUND) LOAF

nutritional analysis per serving (1-inch slice)	
Calories (kcal) 41.7	
Total Fat (g) 0.2	
Cholesterol (mg) 0	
Sodium (mg) 4	
Potassium (mg) 32	

BREAD MACHINE METHOD In the baking pan of a bread machine, place milk, yogurt, gluten, flour and yeast. Bake according to manufacturer's directions. Heat conventional oven to 350°. When bread is baked, remove from bread machine and place in a conventional oven until crusty and brown, about 15 minutes.

CONVENTIONAL METHOD Place a baking stone on the center rack of a cold oven. Heat oven to 425°. In a large bowl, stir yeast into water. When creamy, add milk and yogurt. Mix well. Set aside. In a small bowl, combine gluten with flour and mix in yeast mixture until dough forms. Turn onto a floured board and knead for 5 to 8 minutes, until smooth and elastic. Place in a nonstick pan or in a bowl sprayed with fat-free cooking spray. Cover with plastic wrap and put in a warm place until dough doubles in size, about 1½ hours. Punch down and shape into a large oval. Place on a parchment paper-lined baking sheet. Cover with a damp towel and let dough rise for 45 minutes. Place baking sheet on stone and bake for 10 minutes, spraying oven with water 3 times. Reduce heat to 400° and bake for an additional 25 to 30 minutes. Cool on racks.

NOTE Spraying water into the hot oven creates steam, which helps the bread to develop a thick crust. Be careful not to spray water on the bread loaf.

OATMEAL-RAISIN NUT BREAD

Toasting this fragrant, slightly chewy bread intensifies its flavor. Top with fruit preserves, honey or nonfat cream cheese, or eat plain.

1 1/4 cups warm water

1/4 cup molasses

3 tablespoons frozen apple
    juice concentrate

2 teaspoons cinnamon

1 teaspoon allspice

1/4 cup vital wheat gluten

3/4 cup rolled oats

1 cup oat bran

3/4 cup whole wheat flour

1 1/2 cups all-purpose flour

2 1/2 teaspoons yeast

1/4 cup raisins

1/4 cup chopped walnuts

fat-free cooking spray

1 egg white, slightly beaten

additional rolled oats for
    topping

MAKES 1 (2-POUND) LOAF

nutritional
analysis
per serving
(1-inch slice)

Calories (kcal)	95.1
Total Fat (g)	1.4
Cholesterol (mg)	0
Sodium (mg)	6
Potassium (mg)	147

BREAD MACHINE METHOD In the baking pan of a bread machine, place water, molasses, apple juice concentrate, cinnamon, allspice, gluten, oats, oat bran and flours. Sprinkle yeast on top. Proceed with machine's direction for Raisin Bread. Add the raisins and walnuts at the sound of the tone on the bread machine. Before baking begins, carefully brush top of bread with egg white and sprinkle with rolled oats.

CONVENTIONAL METHOD Preheat oven to 400°. In a large bowl, mix together 1 cup of the water, molasses, apple juice concentrate, cinnamon, allspice and oats. Set aside. In a small bowl, dissolve yeast in remaining 1/4 cup of water. When creamy, add to molasses mixture. Stir in gluten, oat bran and flours. Turn onto a floured board and knead for 5 to 8 minutes until smooth and elastic. Knead in raisins and walnuts. Place in a nonstick pan or in a bowl lightly sprayed with fat-free cooking spray. Cover and let dough rise until doubled in bulk, about 45 to 60 minutes. Punch dough down. Form into an oval loaf and place on a parchment paper-lined baking sheet. Cover and let rise until almost doubled in bulk, about 30 minutes. Brush top of loaf with egg white and sprinkle with rolled oats. Bake until loaf is golden, about 35 to 45 minutes. Remove and cool on a wire rack.

pancakes,
coffee cakes,
eggs & sides

AMERICANS ARE KNOWN for their hearty breakfasts. To keep up with this tradition, we've put together some healthful and hearty recipes. The fat and cholesterol have been removed or modified, while still maintaining a balance of flavor and healthful eating.

CITRUS-KIWI BUTTERMILK PANCAKES

The tangy, sweet flavor of these buttermilk pancakes comes from the tangerine, lemon and kiwi combination. Coconut and lemon cream topped with nuts, tangerine zest and kiwi slices romances the eye as well as the palate.

1 cup silken tofu

3 tablespoons honey

zest and juice of 1 lemon

1 teaspoon coconut syrup, or
　½ teaspoon coconut extract

1 teaspoon lemon syrup, or
　½ teaspoon lemon extract

3 medium tangerines

3 kiwi fruit

1 cup low-fat buttermilk

¼ cup nonfat ricotta cheese

1 cup whole wheat pastry
　flour

½ teaspoon baking soda

1 teaspoon baking powder

4 Brazil nuts, coarsely
　chopped

MAKES 4 SERVINGS

nutritional analysis per serving	
Calories (kcal)	1235.5
Total Fat (g)	98.6
Cholesterol (mg)	10
Sodium (mg)	135
Potassium (mg)	1504
Vitamin C (mg)	107

Using a blender, whip together tofu, 2 tablespoons of the honey, lemon zest, coconut and lemon syrup until smooth. Pour into a serving bowl and set aside. Peel zest from tangerines with a zester or vegetable peeler. Cut into narrow strips, chop and set aside. Juice 1 tangerine and combine with enough lemon juice to make ¼ cup. Set juice aside. Remove white pith from the remaining 2 tangerines, divide into segments, cut into thirds and set aside. Peel, quarter and slice kiwi fruit, and place in a bowl. Pulse buttermilk, tangerine and lemon juice, ricotta and remaining 1 tablespoon honey in a food processor workbowl until smooth. Add flour, baking soda and baking powder. Pulse until well blended. Heat a large nonstick skillet on medium heat until hot. Ladle ¼ cup of batter into a pan for each pancake. Arrange a few pieces of remaining tangerine, tangerine zest and kiwi fruit on each pancake. Cook first side for 2 minutes, or until bubbles begin to form on surface, turn over and cook for 1 minute until cooked through. Serve on a warm platter topped with coconut-lemon syrup, Brazil nuts and remaining tangerine zest. Arrange additional fruit on the side.

NOTE Tofu is available in plastic tubs in the vegetable section of most food markets. It comes in various forms. The "silken" is very soft textured and makes an ideal custard or thick cream substitute. Other textures range from soft to firm. The degree of softness or firmness depends upon the brand. Tofu takes on the flavors of the food it is mixed with and makes a great low-fat cooking substitute.

APRICOT COFFEE CAKE

Fresh apricots combined with fragrant spices and a streusel topping produce a rustic coffee cake. Serve with nonfat cream cheese whipped with non-fat milk and apricot spreadable fruit.

fat-free cooking spray

1½ cups sliced apricots

¾ cup brown sugar, packed

1 teaspoon cinnamon

1 teaspoon cardamom

¼ teaspoon allspice

1 cup all-purpose flour

½ cup whole wheat flour

½ cup oat bran

2 teaspoons baking powder

2 egg whites

1¼ cups "lite" soy milk

2 teaspoons vanilla extract

1 teaspoon almond extract

STREUSEL TOPPING

½ cup finely chopped almonds

⅓ cup wheat germ

2 tablespoons brown sugar, packed

2 teaspoons cinnamon

nutritional analysis per serving

Calories (kcal) 552.3
Total Fat (g) 13.3
Cholesterol (mg) 0
Sodium (mg) 236
Potassium (mg) 797
Vitamin C (mg) 6

Preheat oven to 425°. Spray an 8 x 8 baking pan with fat-free cooking spray. Arrange apricots in bottom of pan. Sprinkle with ¼ cup of the brown sugar, cinnamon, cardamom and allspice. Bake for 5 minutes to partially cook apricots. Remove from oven and set aside. Lower oven to 375°. Combine flours, oat bran, baking powder and remaining ½ cup brown sugar. Set aside. In a large bowl, whisk together egg whites, milk, vanilla and almond extracts. Add flour mixture to liquids and stir until blended. Pour over partially cooked fruit and top with streusel. Bake until golden brown and cooked through, about 30 minutes.

PREPARE STREUSEL by mixing together almonds, wheat germ, brown sugar and cinnamon. Set aside.

MAKES 4 SERVINGS

HEARTY BREAKFAST OMELET

This omelet can be as light or hardy as the cook desires, depending on the filling. A combination of cooked potatoes, tomatoes, button mushrooms, green onions and baby shrimp will satisfy the largest of appetites. Try grated low-fat cheese for a simpler filling.

fat-free cooking spray

2 teaspoons finely chopped
   green onions

¼ cup sliced button
   mushrooms

½ cup cooked baby shrimp

4 large fresh basil leaves,
   cut into thin strips

8 large egg whites

1 large whole egg

2 tablespoons water

white pepper to taste

4 cherry tomatoes, halved for
   garnish

4 small fresh basil sprigs for
   garnish

nutritional analysis per serving	
Calories (kcal)	114.6
Total Fat (g)	2.1
Cholesterol (mg)	72
Sodium (mg)	162
Potassium (mg)	633
Vitamin C (mg)	39

Spray a medium nonstick omelet pan or skillet with fat-free cooking spray. Sauté onions for 1 minute, or until soft. Add mushroom, shrimp and basil and warm through. Transfer to a bowl and keep warm. Wipe out pan and place over medium heat. In a bowl, whisk together egg whites, whole egg, water and pepper. Pour half of the egg mixture into heated pan. Swirl around in pan to even and cook for 1 to 2 minutes, or until partially set. Spread half of the filling over the eggs. Using a spatula, fold the omelet in half. Remove from pan, cut in half and transfer to individual dishes. Repeat with remaining eggs and filling mixture. Garnish each serving with cherry tomato halves and a basil sprig.

MAKES 4 SERVINGS

TRI-COLOR PEPPER FRITATTA

A fritatta is the Italian counterpart to the French omelet. It is easily prepared on the stovetop or baked in the oven. Like the omelet, the combinations are numerous. Even leftovers like thin pasta and risotto, alone or combined with vegetables, beans or bits of meat, become satisfying breakfast fare.

2 links low-fat Italian-style
    turkey sausage
8 large egg whites
1 large whole egg
1 tablespoon water
2 tablespoons extra virgin
    olive oil, or fat-free cooking
    spray
2 cloves garlic, minced
⅓ cup sliced red bell
    peppers
⅓ cup sliced yellow bell
    peppers
⅓ cup sliced green bell
    peppers
2 tablespoons chopped fresh
    basil leaves
½ teaspoon fennel seeds

MAKES 4 SERVINGS

nutritional analysis per serving	
Calories (kcal)	318.3
Total Fat (g)	25.8
Cholesterol (mg)	96
Sodium (mg)	540
Potassium (mg)	333
Vitamin C (mg)	41

Pierce sausage links several times with a knife. Line a flat microwave-safe dish with paper towels. Place sausage links around edge of dish. Microwave on full power, turning once, for 2½ minutes, or until cooked. Alternatively, cook sausage conventionally on stovetop. When cool, remove casing, crumble and set aside.

Preheat oven to 400°. Whisk together egg whites, egg and water. In a 10-inch nonstick skillet with a heat-resistant handle, heat oil over medium heat or spray skillet with fat-free cooking spray. Add garlic and cook until golden. Add peppers and basil. Sauté for 4 minutes, or until peppers are crisp-tender. Stir in fennel seeds and cooked sausage meat, stirring until heated through. Pour in egg mixture and place skillet in oven. Bake until puffy and brown around the edges, about 15 minutes. Divide into 4 portions and serve immediately.

BREAKFAST ALTERNATIVES
Since breakfast is the most important meal of the day, a word should be said about some of the other healthful choices. There are many prepared foods that are low in fat and cholesterol. It is important to read the label for ingredients and nutritional analysis. Fat and over-refined foods find their way into the most unlikely products. The following are some flavorful alternative breakfast suggestions:

WATER BAGELS
Fat-free if prepared in a traditional way. Split, toast and top with nonfat cream cheese, nonfat cottage cheese or ricotta, chopped fresh fruit, fruit spread, chutney, salsa and other sweet or savory condiments.

PREPARED FISH
Pickled herring, gravlax, smoked salmon and caviar are low in fat. The pickled, cured and smoked processes tend to be salty, so watch these if you're on a salt-restricted diet. Use sparingly by mixing with nonfat yogurt, nonfat cream cheese and sour cream.

Serve with crusty all-grain breads and water bagels. Herring is excellent with mixed salad greens and thinly sliced tomatoes. Gravlax and smoked salmon are good companions with room temperature pilaf, chewy wild rice and brown rice combinations.

appetizers & snacks & drinks

APPETIZERS, SNACKS & DRINKS

drinks

Strawberry Yogurt Shake

Breakfast Latte

Breakfast Cappuccino

Spiced Minted Sun Tea

Fruited Green Tea

Soy Drinks

appetizers

Melon and Proscuitto

Bruschetta with Beans and Caviar

Summer Fruit with
Honey-Sesame Dip

Mixed Berry Dipping Sauce

Garlicky Mint Dipping Sauce

Oven-Baked Oysters

Spanish Pepper Crostini
with Saffron

Easy Caponata

Hot and Spicy Yogurt Dip
for Veggies

snacks

Lemon Granita

Strawberry Granita

Melon Granita

Whole Wheat Pizza with
Garlic and Rosemary

Onion Focaccia

Double Apricot Oatmeal Bars

APPETIZERS

As the world grows smaller with increasing technology and travel, our palates become more sophisticated. We have sampled foods from all corners of the earth and are charmed by their flavors and influence. Appetizers in particular reflect these ethnic cooking styles. Today's offerings are healthful and savory, especially when compared to the highly caloric, salty nibbles served in years past. The recipes that follow are simple to prepare, healthful and in most cases have ethnic origins.

Melon and Prosciutto

A most pleasant and classic introduction to a special meal is chilled melon served with prosciutto, lemon and fresh pepper.

1 chilled orange honeydew
   melon, rind removed,
   cut into thin wedges
¼ pound prosciutto, about 16
   paper-thin slices
4 fresh mint sprigs for garnish
2 lemons, cut into wedges
fresh ground pepper to taste

nutritional analysis per serving

Calories (kcal) 179.4
Total Fat (g) 2.9
Cholesterol (mg) 20
Sodium (mg) 799
Potassium (mg) 1099
Vitamin C (mg) 122

Wrap each melon wedge with 1 prosciutto slice. Arrange wrapped melon wedges on 4 chilled salad plates. Decorate with mint sprigs and lemon wedges. Pass the pepper mill.

Makes 4 servings

BRUSCHETTA WITH BEANS AND CAVIAR

Bruschetta or oiled bread had its origins in the peasant household, where a slice of bread was toasted, rubbed with garlic and topped with olive oil and coarse salt. Today bruschetta is a fashionable appetizer. Canned beans and caviar make an unusually elegant, flavorful and nutritious topping.

1 can (15.5 ounces) small
    white beans
2 tablespoons extra virgin
    olive oil
2 tablespoons minced fresh
    sage leaves
1 jar (2 ounces) caviar
1 whole wheat baguette
1 large clove garlic
ground pepper

nutritional
analysis
per serving
(1 bruschetta)

Calories (kcal) 103.8
Total Fat (g) 2.9
Cholesterol (mg) 11
Sodium (mg) 122
Potassium (mg) 248
Vitamin C (mg) 0

Drain, rinse and dry beans with a paper towel. In a serving bowl, lightly mash beans with a fork. Add olive oil and sage and combine. Rinse caviar in a fine sieve under running water until eggs separate from their binding solution. Drain well and spoon caviar over beans. Slice, toast and rub bread with cut garlic. Arrange slices of bread on a serving tray around a serving bowl of beans-caviar mixture. Pass the pepper mill.

MAKES 30 SERVINGS

SUMMER FRUIT WITH HONEY-SESAME DIP

Cubes of fresh fruit threaded on a skewer are served with a nutty honey dip and rice crackers. Fresh ginger juice is available in the produce section of food stores.

2 lemons

1 papaya

1 mango

4 kiwi fruit

2 bananas

1 quart strawberries

16 wooden skewers

spinach leaves for garnish

1 cup honey

2 tablespoons orange juice

½ teaspoon ginger juice

2 tablespoons toasted
    sesame seeds

1 tablespoon chopped fresh
    mint leaves

rice crackers

MAKES 16 FRUIT SKEWERS

nutritional analysis per serving (2-skewer serving with dip)	
Calories (kcal)	241.2
Total Fat (g)	0.9
Cholesterol (mg)	0
Sodium (mg)	8
Potassium (mg)	575
Vitamin C (mg)	136

Cut lemons in half and juice lemons. Place all but 1 tablespoon of the juice into a small spray bottle. Place remaining 1 tablespoon juice into a small deep serving bowl for dip. Set aside. Peel and cube papaya and mango. Peel, halve and quarter kiwi, and slice bananas into 1-inch pieces. Spray cut fruit with lemon juice spray. Thread 10 pieces of cubed, sliced and whole fruit on each skewer. Line a large tray with spinach leaves. Arrange fruit skewers on a tray, leaving the center free for a dip bowl. Set aside. In the serving bowl with lemon juice, whisk in honey, orange and ginger juice, sesame seeds and mint leaves. Mix well. Place a small ladle in a dip bowl. Serve fruit skewers and dip with rice crackers.

NOTE   If time is short, fruit can be cut into larger chunks and served in clusters on a serving platter or in individual bowls. Offer long toothpicks for dipping.

MIXED BERRY DIPPING SAUCE

¾ cup raspberries

¾ cup blackberries

1 tablespoon balsamic vinegar

3 tablespoons confectioners'
   sugar

nutritional
analysis
per serving
(2 tablespoons)

Calories (kcal) 23.9	
Total Fat (g) 0.1	
Cholesterol (mg) 0	
Sodium (mg) 0	
Potassium (mg) 46	
Vitamin C (mg) 6	

MAKES 1 CUP

Puree berries and vinegar with a blender. Add confectioners' sugar and blend until well mixed. Pour into a small bowl and serve with fruit.

GARLICKY MINT DIPPING SAUCE

4 cloves garlic

½ cup packed fresh mint
   leaves

¼ cup champagne vinegar

2 tablespoons light corn syrup

⅔ cup nonfat plain yogurt

nutritional
analysis
per serving
(2 tablespoons)

Calories (kcal) 34.7	
Total Fat (g) 0.2	
Cholesterol (mg) 0	
Sodium (mg) 23	
Potassium (mg) 100	
Vitamin C (mg) 5	

Puree garlic and mint with vinegar with a blender. Add corn syrup and yogurt. Blend on low speed. Pour into a small bowl and serve with fruit.

MAKES 1 CUP

OVEN-BAKED OYSTERS
Use toasted wheat germ combined with sunflower seeds and toasted walnuts to top fresh oysters. Serve with a crisp, dry white wine.

1 jar extra small oysters

2 tablespoons dry white wine

fat-free cooking spray

2 cloves garlic, minced

2 teaspoons chopped fresh
   mint leaves

2 tablespoons chopped fresh
   thyme leaves

¼ cup toasted wheat germ

2 tablespoons sunflower
   seeds

2 tablespoons chopped
   toasted walnuts

2 tablespoons walnut oil

1 seeded whole wheat
   baguette

fresh mint sprigs and lemon
   wedges for garnish

nutritional
analysis
per serving

Calories (kcal)	456.0
Total Fat (g)	15.5
Cholesterol (mg)	2
Sodium (mg)	700
Potassium (mg)	264
Vitamin C (mg)	1

Drain oysters, reserving 3 tablespoons of liquid. Combine oysters, reserved liquid and wine. Cover and marinate in the refrigerator for 20 minutes. Preheat oven to 450°. Spray 12 muffin cups with fat-free cooking spray. Set aside. Pulse garlic, mint leaves, thyme, wheat germ, sunflower seeds and walnuts in a food processor workbowl until finely chopped. Add walnut oil and pulse until well blended. Set aside. Cut baguette into ¼-inch slices. Place 1 slice of bread in each muffin cup, add 1 oyster and top with a little juice. Sprinkle wheat germ mixture evenly over each oyster. Bake until top is golden, about 10 minutes. Carefully remove from cups and place on a serving tray. Garnish with mint sprigs and lemon wedges.

MAKES 4 SERVINGS

Spanish Pepper Crostini with Saffron

This appetizer does not take much time to prepare. It combines the flavor of Spain's peppers and saffron with Italy's capers and polenta. Piquillo peppers are sweet, slightly piquant red peppers that are roasted over wood fires, peeled and packed in their own juice. They are available at specialty food stores.

fat-free cooking spray

¼ cup sherry

1 tablespoon sherry vinegar

⅛ teaspoon saffron powder

1 teaspoon crushed red
    pepper flakes

1 teaspoon sugar

½ teaspoon sweet paprika

½ cup chopped fresh basil
    leaves

1 jar (12 ounces) piquillo
    peppers

2 tubes (1 pound each) firm
    cooked polenta

garlic powder to taste

2 tablespoons rinsed, drained
    large capers

basil sprigs for garnish

nutritional analysis per serving (2 crostini)	
Calories (kcal)	23.5
Total Fat (g)	0.1
Cholesterol (mg)	0
Sodium (mg)	43.2
Potassium (mg)	38
Vitamin C (mg)	1

Preheat broiler. Lightly spray a large baking sheet with fat-free cooking spray. Combine sherry, vinegar, saffron, red pepper flakes, sugar, paprika and basil. Mix well and set aside. Drain peppers and cut into narrow strips with cooking shears. Gently fold pepper strips into liquid mixture. Set aside. Cut each polenta roll into 12 (¼-inch) slices and place on a baking sheet. Lightly spray polenta slices with fat-free cooking spray. Sprinkle with garlic powder. Broil 4 inches from heat source until lightly brown, about 5 minutes on each side. Remove to a wire rack to cool. Coil pepper strips on each polenta slice. Place a few capers in the center. Arrange crostini on a serving platter and garnish with basil sprigs.

Makes 24 crostini

EASY CAPONATA

The amount of eggplant, onions or celery in the caponata can be varied to what you have on hand. Use raisins and pine nuts as accents. Raisins add additional sweetness and pine nuts will increase crunch. The amount of sweet and sour flavor can also be adjusted to your taste.

8 cups cubed eggplant, about
    4 medium eggplants
fat-free cooking spray
2 tablespoons extra virgin
    olive oil or fat-free Italian
    salad dressing
2 medium onions, chopped
½ large head celery,
    chopped
½ cup halved pitted green
    olives
1 cup halved pitted black
    olives
3 tablespoons rinsed, drained
    capers
⅓ cup raisins
¼ cup pine nuts
1 can (8 ounces) tomato
    sauce
½ cup red wine vinegar
3 tablespoons sugar
salt and pepper to taste
French bread baguette slices

MAKES 12 (½ CUP)
SERVINGS

nutritional
analysis
per serving
(½ cup)

Calories (kcal)	195.5
Total Fat (g)	5.3
Cholesterol (mg)	0
Sodium (mg)	469
Potassium (mg)	389
Vitamin C (mg)	7
Vitamin E	

Preheat broiler. On foil-lined baking sheet, place eggplant in a single layer. Lightly spray with fat free cooking spray, turn eggplant and spray again. Place 4 inches below broiler. Broil until light brown and soft, turning once, about 15 to 20 minutes. Turn out into a large bowl. Repeat as many batches as necessary, spraying each batch with fat free cooking spray and turning over once. In a large skillet, heat oil or fat free salad dressing. Cook onion and celery over moderate heat for 12 to 15 minutes, or until celery is no longer crunchy and onion is soft. Stir in olives, capers, raisins, pine nuts, vinegar, sugar and half of the tomato sauce. Mix well. Reduce heat and simmer for 5 minutes. Stir in eggplant and cook for an additional 5 minutes, adding tomato sauce as needed. Caponata should be spreadable but not soupy. Add salt and pepper to taste. Serve at room temperature with baguette slices.

HOT AND SPICY YOGURT DIP FOR VEGGIES

Here is a delicious opportunity to temper cholesterol and reduce high blood pressure with this appetizing dip. Yogurt cheese is drained yogurt with the consistency of a heavy sour cream. It forms the base for this tangy hot and spicy dip. Serve dip with red bell peppers, broccoli florets, carrots, celery and baby turnips.

2 cups nonfat plain yogurt

2 small fresh jalapeño
    peppers

2 tablespoons water

2 cloves garlic, chopped

1 teaspoon cumin seeds

1 teaspoon fennel seeds

2 teaspoons coriander seeds

½ cup chopped fresh cilantro

¼ cup chopped fresh mint
    leaves

1 teaspoon grated lime zest

1 tablespoon lime juice

½ cup unsalted dry-roasted
    peanuts

1 tablespoon chopped fresh
    chives or green onion tops
    for garnish

red bell pepper strips, broccoli
    florets, carrot and celery
    strips and turnip slices

nutritional analysis per serving
(3 tablespoons)

Calories (kcal) 97.5
Total Fat (g) 4.9
Cholesterol (mg) 1
Sodium (mg) 48
Potassium (mg) 313
Vitamin C (mg) 35

In a fine mesh sieve, drain yogurt over a bowl. Cover and refrigerate for several hours or overnight. Wearing rubber gloves, seed and devein peppers, discarding seeds and membrane. Cut into small pieces and place in a blender container with water, garlic and cumin, fennel and coriander seeds. Blend until smooth and pour into a serving bowl. Drain chilled yogurt, discarding liquid. Add yogurt to pepper mixture. Fold in cilantro, mint leaves, lime zest, juice and peanuts. When ready to serve, top with chives and surround with cut vegetables.

MAKES 1½ CUPS

HEALTHFUL SNACKS CONTRIBUTE to good health and satisfy the desire for a little something between meals. One of the major reasons diets fail is that they are too rigid or leave you feeling hungry. This sometimes leads to overeating at mealtime. Fruit, vegetables, nuts and seeds, breads, drinks and even whole grain cookie bars all make great snacks. These snacks satisfy hunger, provide energy and maintain good health.

LEMON GRANITA

Summertime in the city can be sweltering. Recollections of cooling off with an Italian ice brings back fond childhood memories. Its cool, tangy flavor makes it luscious. Granita is best eaten within the week, since it tends to harden in the freezer.

2 cups water
1 cup sugar
1 cup lemon juice
2 tablespoons grated lemon
 zest

nutritional analysis per serving

Calories (kcal) 208.8
Total Fat (g) 0
Cholesterol (mg) 0
Sodium (mg) 5
Potassium (mg) 81
Vitamin C (mg) 32

MAKES 4 SERVINGS

In a 2-quart saucepan, bring water and sugar to a boil for 5 minutes. Remove from heat and cool to room temperature. When cool, stir in lemon juice and zest. Pour into an ice cube tray. Freeze 3 to 4 hours. Granita should be frozen but slushy. If granita freezes hard, break up with a fork and briefly whirl with a blender until smooth.

Strawberry Granita

1 cup water
½ cup sugar
2 cups fresh strawberry puree
2 tablespoons lemon juice

nutritional analysis per serving	
Calories (kcal)	121.0
Total Fat (g)	0.3
Cholesterol (mg)	0
Sodium (mg)	3
Potassium (mg)	134
Vitamin C (mg)	46

Makes 4 servings

Proceed as directed for *Lemon Granita*.

Melon Granita

Exotic ices can be made with bottled nut and fruit syrups. Unsweetened varieties are also available. Try such combinations as almond-vanilla, hazelnut-raspberry and macadamia nut-mango.

Makes 4 servings

Follow *Lemon Granita* recipe, but substitute pureed cantaloupe, honeydew, Crenshaw or casaba melons for lemon zest. If melons are ripe and sweet, extra sugar may not be necessary. Use 3 cups melon puree and 2 tablespoons lemon juice and proceed as directed.

Whole Wheat Pizza with Garlic and Rosemary

Chewy pizza and focaccia make great-tasting, high-energy snacks. Garlic is the choice for its pungent flavor and multi-medicinal properties. If you're using a bread machine, prepare with the dough cycle to mix and knead dough. Follow manufacturer's directions or use the method below.

2½ teaspoons active dry yeast

1½ cups warm water

1 cup whole wheat flour

3 cups all-purpose flour

fat-free cooking spray

2 cups thinly sliced garlic, about 14 cloves garlic

¼ cup chopped fresh rosemary

extra-coarse sea salt to taste

Makes 2 (10-inch) pizzas

nutritional analysis per serving (¼ pizza)

Calories (kcal) 564.0
Total Fat (g) 2.4
Cholesterol (mg) 0
Sodium (mg) 20
Potassium (mg) 579
Vitamin C (mg) 24

In a large bowl, dissolve yeast into water. In a separate bowl, combine flours. When yeast mixture is creamy, beat in flour mixture. Knead dough on a lightly floured surface until smooth and elastic, about 8 to 10 minutes. Place dough in a bowl lightly sprayed with fat-free cooking spray. Cover with plastic wrap to rise in a warm place until puffy, but not doubled, about 1 hour. Preheat oven to 500º. While oven is still cool, place a baking stone on the center rack and preheat stone for 30 minutes before baking pizza. When dough is ready, press down, knead briefly and divide into 2 pieces. Roll or press each half into a lightly sprayed 10-inch pizza pan. With your knuckles, dimple dough and spray with fat-free cooking spray. Cover with garlic slices and rosemary. Lightly spray pizza again with fat-free cooking spray. Lower heat to 450º. Place pizza pans directly on preheated stone. Bake pizza until crust is brown and pizza is cooked through, about 15 to 18 minutes. Enjoy at room temperature with a few grindings of sea salt if permissible.

Onion Focaccia

Focaccia takes on a French flavor with sweet red onions and herbs de Provence. Cooked wheat berries, kneaded in before the first rise, gives the crust extraordinary chewiness. Makes a great afternoon snack with a glass of nonfat milk or red wine.

2½ teaspoons active dry yeast

1½ cups warm water

1 cup whole wheat flour

3 cups all-purpose flour

1 cup cooked wheat berries

fat-free cooking spray

2 cups thinly sliced red onions, about 1 large onion

½ cup herbs de Provence

Makes 8 servings

nutritional analysis per serving (¼ focaccia)

Calories (kcal) 307.8
Total Fat (g) 1.3
Cholesterol (mg) 0
Sodium (mg) 4
Potassium (mg) 167
Vitamin C (mg) 1

Combine yeast with ¼ cup of the water. Set aside until creamy. In a large bowl, stir together flours. Make a well in center of mixture and gradually pour in remaining 1¼ cups warm water and yeast mixture, stirring well with a wooden spoon. On a floured surface, knead dough until smooth and elastic. Knead in wheat berries. Place in a bowl lightly sprayed with fat-free cooking spray, cover and let rise for 1½ to 2 hours, until doubled in bulk. Preheat oven to 500°. While oven is still cool, place a baking stone on the bottom rack and heat for 30 minutes. When dough is ready, punch down, divide in half and press each half into a sprayed pizza pan. Divide onions and herbs de Provence evenly between 2 focaccia. Lightly spray each focaccia with fat-free cooking spray. Place pans directly on baking stones and bake until crust is brown and focaccia is cooked through, about 15 to 20 minutes.

DOUBLE APRICOT OATMEAL BARS

Apricot puree substitutes for oil and apricot conserve provides the filling for this spicy, crumbly bar cookie. A small square satisfies the "sweet tooth" urge, and provides fiber, vitamins and minerals.

fat-free cooking spray

1 cup whole wheat flour

2 cups quick-cooking rolled oats

1 cup oat bran

1 tablespoon baking powder

1 tablespoon cinnamon

1 teaspoon nutmeg

½ teaspoon ground ginger

4 large egg whites

½ cup pureed apricot

1 cup brown sugar, packed

½ cup nonfat milk

2 teaspoons vanilla extract

1 cup apricot preserves, warmed in microwave

½ cup chopped walnuts

2 tablespoons cinnamon

2 tablespoons sugar

nutritional analysis per serving (1 bar)	
Calories (kcal)	131.2
Total Fat (g)	2.3
Cholesterol (mg)	0
Sodium (mg)	130
Potassium (mg)	139
Vitamin C (mg)	1
Vitamin E	

Preheat oven to 350°. Lightly spray a 9 x 13 pan with fat-free cooking spray. Combine wheat flour, oats, oat bran, baking powder, cinnamon, nutmeg and ginger. Mix well and set aside. In a large bowl, whisk together egg whites, pureed apricot, brown sugar, milk and vanilla extract. Fold flour mixture into egg white mixture until well blended. Spread half of the mixture in the prepared baking pan. Top with softened apricot preserves and chopped walnuts. Spread remaining mixture over filling. Combine cinnamon and sugar and dust top. Bake until golden brown and cooked through, about 25 to 30 minutes. Cool slightly and cut into 24 bars.

NOTE   Match a fruit preserve with a pureed fruit and create an assortment of different tasting oatmeal bars.

MAKES 24 BARS

THERE ARE A VARIETY of beverages to choose from that are good-tasting and nutritious. Fruit juice, nonfat milk, yogurt-based drinks, soy drinks, herbal and fruit teas and even coffee can be healthful!

Espresso grinds and green teas do contain caffeine, so enjoy them in moderation. Always read labels carefully when purchasing packaged drinks. The nutritional analysis identifies potential problem areas by listing ingredients and percentages of fat and cholesterol.

STRAWBERRY YOGURT SHAKE
Fruit and yogurt combined makes a frosty, flavorful energy booster. For variety, try apricots, peaches, plums, mango, papaya, bananas, melons, berries or pears.

½ cup nonfat plain yogurt
1 teaspoon vanilla or almond
    extract
½ cup sliced strawberries
5 ice cubes

nutritional
analysis
per serving

Calories (kcal) 90.3
Total Fat (g) 0.5
Cholesterol (mg) 2
Sodium (mg) 91
Potassium (mg) 413
Vitamin C (mg) 43

MAKES 1 SERVING

Blend yogurt, vanilla extract, strawberries and ice cubes until smooth and frothy, about 30 seconds.

VARIATION   Fruit shakes can also be made using unflavored soy milk instead of yogurt. Follow the Strawberry Yogurt Shake recipe and substitute soy milk for yogurt.

BREAKFAST LATTE

Espresso brewed in an inexpensive coffee pot stars in this simple-to-make latte. Enriched with instant nonfat powdered milk, this breakfast latte is sure to please.

4 cups nonfat milk
1 cup instant nonfat
   powdered milk
4 espresso-sized cups brewed
   espresso or decaffeinated
   espresso

Pour 1 cup of the milk into each of 4 tempered glass mugs. Microwave each cup on full power for 1 minute 55 seconds. Remove from microwave and whisk ¼ cup of the powdered milk into each mug. Whisk until foam reaches almost to the top of the mug. Slowly pour espresso down one side of each mug under the foamed milk. Serve immediately. The natural sugars in the milk make extra sweetening unnecessary.

MAKES 4 SERVINGS

BREAKFAST CAPPUCCINO

Start your day off right with a flavorful combination of espresso and cinnamon.

2 cups nonfat milk
4 espresso-sized cups brewed
   espresso or decaffeinated
   espresso
2 teaspoons cinnamon
sugar cubes

Pour milk into a 4-cup glass measuring pitcher. Microwave on full power for 4 to 5 minutes, until hot but not boiling. Remove from the microwave and whisk until double in volume. Fill a cappuccino cup halfway with brewed espresso. Spoon foamed milk to top of drink, and sprinkle with ¼ teaspoon of the cinnamon. Repeat for remaining drinks. Serve with sugar cubes.

MAKES 4 SERVINGS

SPICED MINTED SUN TEA

Add some sunshine to your afternoon with a cool, fresh glass of mint tea.

1 quart bottled water
4 tea bags, spice flavored
2 fresh lemon mint sprigs
4 lemon wedges

nutritional analysis per serving

Calories (kcal)	11.0
Total Fat (g)	0.1
Cholesterol (mg)	0
Sodium (mg)	11
Potassium (mg)	179
Vitamin C (mg)	21

MAKES 4 SERVINGS

In a 2-quart glass jar, combine water, tea bags and mint sprigs. Place in the sun for several hours, or until tea has steeped sufficiently to a deep amber color. Pour over ice cubes and serve with lemon wedges.

FRUITED GREEN TEA

Fruit juice naturally sweetens green tea and imparts a pleasant fruitiness. Citrus combinations are tangy, while tropical juices are milder in flavor.

4 cups bottled water
3½ teaspoons loose green
tea, or 4 tea bags
½ cup tangerine or orange
juice

nutritional analysis per serving

Calories (kcal)	24.3
Total Fat (g)	0.1
Cholesterol (mg)	0
Sodium (mg)	13
Potassium (mg)	339
Vitamin C (mg)	10

MAKES 4 SERVINGS

Heat water over high heat until bubbling. Pour into a heated teapot. Add tea and steep for 3 to 4 minutes. Add tangerine juice. Serve warm or over ice.

SOY DRINKS

Soy milk is the liquid produced when soybeans are boiled, ground and strained. It is available in cartons like cow's milk, but contains little fat and cholesterol. Because of the protein, it makes a satisfying, quick-energy snack. Several suppliers offer unflavored, vanilla and chocolate soy milks. Each brand varies somewhat in taste, so try them to determine which one is right for you. Here are some soy drink combinations:

HEAT chocolate-flavored soy milk. Stir in ground cinnamon, cardamom, nutmeg, ginger or cloves for a spicy, cold weather drink.

BLEND chocolate-flavored soy milk, low-fat chocolate ice cream and chocolate syrup for a nourishing low-fat milkshake.

COMBINE vanilla soy milk with fresh fruit slices or fruit purees. Blend with ice cubes for a frosty drink.

STIR almond extract into unflavored soy milk. Serve over ice and garnish with mint.

salads & soups & sides

SALADS SOUPS & SIDES

salads

Avocado Wheat Berry Salad

Carrot Salad with Ginger

Fruity Cabbage Slaw

Lemon and Orange Salad

Savory Spinach Salad

Potato Salad with Herbs

soups

Succotash Chowder

Creamy Asparagus Soup

Rainy Day Mung Bean Soup

sides

Brown Rice and Peas

Green Beans Two Ways

    Green Beans Oregano

    Green Beans with Lemon

Stuffed Artichokes

Sweet Potatoes with Bourbon

Garlic Mashed Potatoes

Kasha Pilaf

Balsamic Baked Onions

SALADS, SOUPS & SIDES represent a sampling of

healthful foods. The vegetables and fruits used here contain foods cited in the text as being beneficial to a healthy heart. Enjoy avocado, carrots, corn, citrus, beans, squash, nuts and grains, and garlic flavorings, onions, spices and herbs in your next salad, soup or side dish.

Color, taste and texture can also give salads an added appeal. Try the *Savory Spinach Salad* with vegetables, fruit, cheese, nuts and seeds.

Refrigerate meat and poultry-based soups so the fat can be removed before serving. Creamed soups like the *Creamy Asparagus Soup* can be prepared with grated potato instead of fatty cream. When whipped in the blender, potato becomes the thickening agent instead of cream.

Side dishes of vegetables, fruit, grains or a combination of all three are always a good choice. Roasting in a hot oven brings out the flavor in vegetables by caramelizing the sugars. A touch of wine vinegar like the *Balsamic Baked Onions* works magic on root vegetables, onions and garlic. Broaden your culinary horizon by including less common beans, nuts and grains in your vegetable cookery. A variety of healthful foods can be the spark that brings pleasure back to the dinner table.

Avocado Wheat Berry Salad

Wheat berry is the whole kernel of wheat with the inedible hull removed. Its chewy texture and nutty flavor is similar to that of wild and brown rice combined. It's available in the bulk bins of health food stores.

1 cup wheat berries

3 cups water

3 tablespoons fat-free vinaigrette

2 tablespoons melted red pepper jelly

¼ cup lemon juice or combined lemon and orange juice

2 tablespoons chopped green onions

1 clove garlic, minced

½ cup chopped red bell pepper

½ cup chopped yellow bell pepper

½ cup chopped zucchini

1 medium avocado, sliced

5 cups watercress leaves or arugula

¼ cup chopped fresh lemon mint leaves

nutritional analysis per serving

Calories (kcal) 261.4
Total Fat (g) 9.0
Cholesterol (mg) 0
Sodium (mg) 174
Potassium (mg) 603
Vitamin C (mg) 83

On a stovetop, bring berries to a boil. Lower heat and cook for 1 hour, or until tender and water has evaporated. Whisk together vinaigrette, pepper jelly and lemon juice. Add onion, garlic, reserved wheat berries, red and yellow peppers and zucchini. Mix well. Fold in avocado, watercress and lemon mint leaves. Gently mix, taking care not to mash avocado or bruise watercress. Serve at room temperature.

Makes 4 servings

CARROT SALAD WITH GINGER

Carrots and ginger marry well together, bringing out the best flavors of each. Select slender young carrots, fresh spring ginger, golden raisins and spring onions for best results.

1 cup golden raisins

1 cup orange juice

1 tablespoon grated orange zest

1-inch slice fresh ginger, peeled and grated

2 tablespoons mango chutney

1 cup nonfat plain yogurt

1 teaspoon lemon juice

2 cups cut cooked carrots, in 1/8-inch rounds

5 cups torn romaine lettuce

1 tablespoon finely sliced green onions for garnish

1/4 cup chopped unsalted dry-roasted peanuts for garnish

nutritional analysis per serving	
Calories (kcal) 199.7	
Total Fat (g) 3.6	
Cholesterol (mg) 1	
Sodium (mg) 76	
Potassium (mg) 806	
Vitamin C (mg) 43	

In a large salad bowl, combine raisins and orange juice. Cover and soak for 20 minutes. Add orange zest, ginger, chutney, yogurt, lemon juice and carrots. Gently mix until dressing is well blended. Fold in lettuce. Garnish salad with finely chopped green onions and peanuts.

MAKES 6 SERVINGS

FRUITY CABBAGE SLAW

This variation on cole slaw with its sweet tart taste and nutty crunchiness complements steamed or microwaved fish. For an unusual salad entrée, serve with nonfat ricotta cheese and seeded rye bread.

2 cloves garlic, minced

1 tablespoon hazelnut oil

2 tablespoons raspberry
   vinegar

½ teaspoon salt

several grindings of black
   pepper

¼ cup dried cranberries

1 medium navel orange,
   peeled

7 cups finely shredded
   cabbage

¼ cup halved hazelnuts

nutritional analysis per serving	
Calories (kcal)	130.3
Total Fat (g)	8.2
Cholesterol (mg)	0
Sodium (mg)	290
Potassium (mg)	418
Vitamin C (mg)	85
Vitamin E	

In a large salad bowl, mix garlic with oil, vinegar, salt, pepper and cranberries. Divide orange into segments. Cut segments into 1-inch pieces and add to mixture. Fold in cabbage and mix well. Sprinkle with hazelnuts. Marinate for 20 minutes before serving.

MAKES 4 SERVINGS

LEMON AND ORANGE SALAD

When a refreshing salad is needed to round out a rich dinner, nothing beats this salad. Its citrus flavor is complimented by sweet fennel, while the bitter greens form a crisp base.

3 small lemons

4 large navel oranges

¼ cup fat-free vinaigrette

2 tablespoons chopped fresh
   oregano leaves

1 large oval head fresh fennel

salt and freshly ground
   pepper to taste

8 cups shredded mixed
   endive and escarole leaves

1 cup thinly sliced radishes,
   optional

MAKES 6 SERVINGS

nutritional analysis per serving	
Calories (kcal)	88.2
Total Fat (g)	0.6
Cholesterol (mg)	0
Sodium (mg)	191
Potassium (mg)	678
Vitamin C (mg)	108

Grate enough zest from lemons and oranges to make 1 tablespoon of lemon zest and 2 tablespoons of orange zest. Place in a large salad bowl. Peel fruit, cut in half and slice into ¼-inch slices, saving the juice. Place cut fruit and juice in a salad bowl. Add vinaigrette and oregano. Cut anise in half and slice into ¼-inch crosswise slices. Add anise and sprinkle with salt and pepper. Mix well. Fold in endive, escarole and radish slices. Leftover salad may be covered and refrigerated for the next day.

SAVORY SPINACH SALAD

Fresh spinach combined with fruit, nuts, seeds and cheese produces a satisfying luncheon dish. Serve with crusty whole wheat or seeded seven grain bread for extra fiber.

2 cloves garlic, minced

1 tablespoon hazelnut oil, or
   3 tablespoons fat-free
   vinaigrette

2 tablespoons raspberry
   vinegar

½ teaspoon salt

several grindings of black
   pepper

1 cup sliced fresh fennel or
   anise

1 cup seeded, quartered red
   globe grapes

1 pear, sliced

4 ounces smoked Gouda
   cheese, thinly sliced

8 cups loosely packed
   spinach leaves

¼ cup mixed hazelnuts and
   sunflower seeds

additional black pepper,
   optional

nutritional analysis per serving	
Calories (kcal)	264.2
Total Fat (g)	16.5
Cholesterol (mg)	32
Sodium (mg)	600
Potassium (mg)	939
Vitamin C (mg)	38
Vitamin E	

In a large salad bowl, mix garlic with hazelnut oil or fat-free vinaigrette, vinegar, salt and pepper. Add fennel, grapes, pear and cheese. Mix well. Fold in spinach leaves. Divide among 4 chilled plates, topping each serving with nut and seed mixture. Pass the pepper mill.

MAKES 4 SERVINGS

POTATO SALAD WITH HERBS

The success of this potato salad depends on the variety and size of the potatoes. Choose small, evenly sized red, purple, white rose and yellow Finn potatoes, usually available at farmers' markets in the early summer or fall.

2 pounds assorted red, white, yellow and purple small potatoes

2 tablespoons fat-free mayonnaise

2 tablespoons raspberry vinegar

¼ cup dry white wine

¼ cup dried raspberries

1 tablespoon chopped shallot

1 teaspoons fresh oregano

1 teaspoons fresh rosemary

1 teaspoons fresh flat-leaf parsley

1 head curly green-leaf lettuce for garnish

nutritional analysis per serving	
Calories (kcal) 137.1	
Total Fat (g) 0.3	
Cholesterol (mg) 0	
Sodium (mg) 74	
Potassium (mg) 865	
Vitamin C (mg) 32	

Scrub potatoes but do not peel. Cook potatoes in a large saucepan with water. Boil for 15 to 18 minutes, or until tender. Set aside. In a large bowl, whisk together fat-free mayonnaise, vinegar, wine, shallot, oregano, rosemary and parsley. Set aside. When potatoes are cooked, rinse under cold water and peel. Cut potatoes in half and fold in raspberry-herb dressing, until potatoes are well coated. Spoon into a lettuce-lined serving platter. Place potato salad on platter and serve.

MAKES 6 SERVINGS

Succotash Chowder

Corn and lima beans combined with potatoes and Middle Eastern spices produce a wholesome chunky soup. Serve with lavash or oven-roasted cumin-flavored flat bread.

½ large jalapeño pepper

1 medium onion, finely chopped

2 stalks celery, finely chopped

2 carrots, finely chopped

1 leek, white part only, finely chopped

6 cups vegetable stock

1 teaspoon paprika

1 teaspoon ground cumin

¾ teaspoon ground coriander

½ teaspoon allspice

2 russet potatoes, peeled and chopped

1 package frozen whole corn

1 package frozen baby lima beans

1 can (12 ounces) evaporated skim milk

1 round (10-inch) flat bread

nutritional analysis per serving

Calories (kcal)	218.9
Total Fat (g)	1.0
Cholesterol (mg)	2
Sodium (mg)	719
Potassium (mg)	984
Vitamin C (mg)	34

Remove seeds and ribs from jalapeño pepper and chop. To save time, chop vegetables with a food processor. In an 8-quart stockpot over medium heat, cook onion, celery, carrots, leek and jalapeño pepper in 1 cup of the vegetable stock for 15 minutes, or until wilted. Stir frequently to prevent sticking. Add remaining 5 cups vegetable stock, paprika, ¾ teaspoon of the cumin, and coriander, allspice, potatoes, corn and lima beans. Bring to a boil. Cover and simmer for 20 minutes until vegetables are cooked and soup is fragrant. Just before serving, stir in milk. Preheat oven to 400º. Lightly dust flat bread with remaining ¼ teaspoon of cumin. Place on a baking sheet. Bake until lightly toasted, about 8 minutes. Serve with chowder.

NOTE To avoid curdling, do not boil once milk is added. Reheat over low heat to just below the boiling point.

Makes 6 servings

CREAMY ASPARAGUS SOUP

Vegetarian chicken broth powder, available at health food stores, is a soy protein product. It forms a flavorful base for soup made mostly from asparagus stalk scraps with a few tips for garnish. Grated potato adds richness without the fat and calories of cream.

1 small leek, 1-inch thick,
   washed and thinly sliced
2 tablespoons water
¼ cup vegetarian chicken
   broth powder
4 cups boiling water
1 pound fresh asparagus
   stalks, about 6 cups
1 medium potato, peeled and
   coarsely grated
salt and white pepper to taste
several grindings of nutmeg
1 cup cooked asparagus tips

MAKES 4 SERVINGS

nutritional analysis per serving

Calories (kcal)	96.4
Total Fat (g)	0.8
Cholesterol (mg)	0
Sodium (mg)	797
Potassium (mg)	769
Vitamin C (mg)	40
Vitamin E	

In a large microwave-safe bowl, cook leek with water, cover and cook on full power for 2 minutes until aromatic. Combine broth powder with boiling water and whisk into leek mixture. Add asparagus stalks and potato. Cover bowl and continue cooking on full power for 5 minutes until stalks are tender and potato nearly dissolves. Remove from oven and cool slightly. Carefully ladle soup into a food processor workbowl and pulse in batches until smooth and creamy. Stir in salt, pepper, nutmeg and asparagus tips. Serve immediately.

VARIATION   Broccoli, carrots, celery, fennel, cauliflower or almost any vegetable can be substituted for the asparagus. Merely adjust cooking times and seasoning.

RAINY DAY MUNG BEAN SOUP

Mung beans are small dried beans that are usually used to grow bean sprouts. On their own they have a sweet, delicate flavor and are ideal for a quick, rainy day soup.

⅓ cup chopped smoked
   turkey thigh meat or
   very lean ham
¾ cup chopped onions
3 cloves garlic, chopped
¾ teaspoon crushed red
   pepper flakes
½ cup chopped celery
¼ cup chopped leeks
1 cup chopped carrots
¾ cup chopped parsnips
1 cup mung beans
4 quarts water
1 teaspoon thyme
1 teaspoon marjoram
3 tablespoons low-sodium
   soy sauce
¼ cup chopped fresh flat-leaf
   parsley

MAKES 4 SERVINGS

nutritional analysis per serving

Calories (kcal)	283.1
Total Fat (g)	2.4
Cholesterol (mg)	13
Sodium (mg)	561
Potassium (mg)	1116
Vitamin C (mg)	22

In an 8-quart stockpot over medium heat, brown bacon, onions, garlic and red pepper flakes, stirring frequently. Add celery, leeks, carrots, parsnips and mung beans. Cook for 3 minutes, stirring constantly. Add water, thyme, marjoram and soy sauce. Cover, bring to a boil, lower heat and simmer for 30 to 35 minutes until beans are tender. Stir in parsley before serving.

BROWN RICE AND PEAS

Using aromatic brown rice instead of arborio rice gives it a pleasing chewy texture. Always use fresh peas and good-quality beef broth. If your fat is restricted, use fat-free Italian salad dressing instead of butter. The salad dressing will make the flavors of this dish more robust.

¼ cup unsalted butter or fat-free Italian salad dressing

¼ cup finely chopped onions

4 cups freshly shelled peas

½ teaspoon salt

1 teaspoon sugar

1 can (12 ounces) defatted low-sodium beef broth

3 cans water

1 cup brown rice

¼ cup chopped fresh flat-leaf parsley

½ cup grated Parmesan cheese

nutritional analysis per serving	
Calories (kcal)	476.2
Total Fat (g)	18
Cholesterol (mg)	42
Sodium (mg)	1043
Potassium (mg)	672
Vitamin C (mg)	63

In a large stockpot, heat butter or fat-free salad dressing and onions over medium heat, until onions soften and begin to brown. Add peas, salt and sugar. Cook for 3 minutes, stirring constantly. Add half of the broth and 2 cups of the water. Cover and simmer for 10 minutes. Stir in rice, remaining half can of broth and remaining 1 cup water. Cover and simmer for 45 minutes, or until rice and peas are cooked and liquid is almost absorbed. Stir in parsley and cheese. Serve immediately.

MAKES 4 SERVINGS

Green Beans Two Ways

Green beans are everyone's favorite green vegetable. These two presentations showcase green beans with different seasoning. If you're on a restricted diet, use a fat-free dressing substitute for the oil and butter. If you do include the oil or butter, it amounts to ½ teaspoon of fat per serving.

Green Beans Oregano

1 pound green beans
2 tablespoons extra-virgin
    olive oil or fat-free Italian
    salad dressing
1 clove garlic, slivered
1 tablespoon chopped fresh
    oregano
salt and freshly ground
    pepper to taste

Makes 6 servings

nutritional
analysis
per serving

Calories (kcal) 65.4
Total Fat (g) 4.6
Cholesterol (mg) 0
Sodium (mg) 27
Potassium (mg) 168
Vitamin C (mg) 36

In a large pot, bring 2 quarts of water to a boil. Add beans and blanch for 5 minutes, or until crisp-tender. Drain and keep warm. Beans will continue to cook so be sure not to over cook initially. In a large microwave-safe bowl, heat oil or fat-free salad dressing and garlic on full power for 1 minute, or until garlic is fragrant but not brown. Discard garlic. Fold in beans and oregano, mixing well. Add salt and pepper to taste. Serve warm.

GREEN BEANS WITH LEMON

1 pound green beans

2 tablespoons unsalted butter
    or fat-free vinaigrette

2 tablespoons thinly sliced
    shallot

2 tablespoons chopped fresh
    parsley

salt and pepper to taste

juice of ½ lemon, or to taste

MAKES 6 SERVINGS

nutritional
analysis
per serving

| Calories (kcal) 63.5 |
| Total Fat (g) 4.2 |
| Cholesterol (mg) 11 |
| Sodium (mg) 28 |
| Potassium (mg) 184 |
| Vitamin C (mg) 17 |

Cook beans as instructed in *Green Bean Oregano*, page 142. In a large skillet, heat butter until foaming or salad dressing until warm. Lower heat and sauté sliced shallot until tender. Fold in beans and parsley, mixing well. Add salt and pepper to taste. Squeeze lemon juice over just before serving.

Stuffed Artichokes

Who would guess that these garlicky artichokes were stuffed with oat bran, wheat germ and whole wheat bread? Use fat-free salad dressing as a substitute for extra virgin olive oil if you have a restricted diet. This side dish goes well with baked or steamed fish or alone as a separate course.

4 medium to large fresh
  artichokes
1 lemon, halved
2 cups water
½ cup packed fresh flat-leaf
  parsley
¼ cup fresh oregano leaves
1 tablespoon chopped fresh
  mint leaves
4 cloves garlic
2 tablespoons oat bran
2 tablespoons toasted wheat
  germ
1 ½ cups toasted whole wheat
  breadcrumbs
1 teaspoon grated lemon zest
¼ cup plus 2 tablespoons dry
  white wine
2 tablespoons olive oil or fat-
  free Italian salad dressing
lemon wedges
fresh oregano sprigs for
  garnish

Makes 4 servings

nutritional analysis per serving	Calories (kcal) 331.4
	Total Fat (g) 10.6
	Cholesterol (mg) 0
	Sodium (mg) 464
	Potassium (mg) 844
	Vitamin C (mg) 48

Wash artichokes. Rap artichokes sharply on a countertop to slightly open leaves. Cut off stems and remove fuzzy choke from center. Rub cut surfaces of artichoke with 1 lemon half. Squeeze juice from the other lemon half into a large bowl. Add water and mix well. Place artichokes and stems in lemon water. Set aside. Mince together parsley, oregano, mint and garlic until well blended. Combine minced herb mixture, oat bran, wheat germ, breadcrumbs, zest, ¼ cup of the wine and oil or fat-free salad dressing. Stir until mixture comes together. If too dry, add extra wine. To fill each artichoke, gently open leaves and place ¼ to ½ teaspoon of crumb mixture into each leaf. Press to close. Continue until each leaf is full. When all artichokes are stuffed, place in a 4-quart saucepan. Pour lemon water into a pan at a depth of 1 ¾ inches. Drizzle remaining wine evenly over the top of each artichoke. Bring to a boil, lower heat, cover and simmer for 40 minutes, or until a leaf pulls away easily. Serve with lemon wedges and garnish with oregano sprigs.

SWEET POTATOES WITH BOURBON

Traditional candied sweet potatoes are enriched with the flavors of bourbon and pecans. The combination of brown sugar and dark corn syrup adds a creaminess without added fat or cholesterol. This dish is too good to save for holiday dinners.

4 large sweet potatoes or
    yams
¼ cup dark corn syrup
1 cup brown sugar, packed
1 teaspoon balsamic vinegar
½ cup bourbon
1 teaspoon cinnamon
½ teaspoon ground ginger
½ teaspoon allspice
¼ teaspoon ground cloves
½ cup coarsely chopped
    pecans
½ cup coarsely chopped
    walnuts

nutritional
analysis
per serving

Calories (kcal)	392.1
Total Fat (g)	12.3
Cholesterol (mg)	0
Sodium (mg)	47
Potassium (mg)	405
Vitamin C (mg)	20

Preheat oven to 350º. Boil sweet potatoes for 15 minutes, or until crisp-tender. Peel and cut sweet potatoes into ½-inch rounds. Set aside. In a shallow ovenproof casserole dish or skillet, mix together corn syrup, brown sugar and balsamic vinegar. Microwave on high for 3 minutes until bubbling. Stir well. Mix in bourbon, cinnamon, ginger, allspice and cloves. Arrange sweet potato slices with pecans and walnuts in casserole dish. Gently turn with a spatula to coat potatoes and nuts with sauce. Bake for 30 minutes, spooning sauce over sweet potatoes every 10 minutes.

MAKES 6 SERVINGS

GARLIC MASHED POTATOES

Garlic mashed potatoes are quite popular nation-wide in bistro-style restaurants. This version uses 1 garlic clove for each potato and cooks them in low-fat, low-sodium chicken broth for extra flavor and richness. Sprinkle with chopped chives for a colorful presentation.

8 medium red potatoes with
  skins, quartered
8 large cloves garlic, crushed
1 can (14½ ounces)
  defatted low-sodium
  chicken broth
¼ cup chopped fresh chives
  for garnish

MAKES 4 SERVINGS

nutritional
analysis
per serving

Calories (kcal) 194.0
Total Fat (g) 0.3
Cholesterol (mg) 0
Sodium (mg) 228
Potassium (mg) 1310
Vitamin C (mg) 48

In a 4-quart saucepan, combine potatoes, garlic and chicken broth. Bring to a boil. Lower heat to medium and cook for 20 minutes, or until potatoes pierce easily with a fork. Drain and reserve cooking liquid. Mash using a sturdy whisk. Whisk in reserved cooking liquid, 1 tablespoon at a time, until potatoes are light and fluffy. Serve immediately and garnish with chopped chives.

KASHA PILAF
Kasha is a mild-tasting, somewhat chewy grain. Its flavor comes alive when accented with a lemon, mustard and dill dressing. This version is delightful served either hot, cold or at room temperature.

¼ cup chopped shallots
¼ cup chopped celery
½ cup chopped yellow onions
½ cup chopped green onions
4 cloves garlic, minced
1 cup kasha
½ cup chopped fresh dill
2 cups low-sodium vegetable
    broth
2 tablespoons Dijon mustard
½ cup Chablis
2 teaspoons garlic powder
¼ cup grated lemon zest
additional chopped fresh dill
    for garnish

nutritional
analysis
per serving

Calories (kcal) 144.7
Total Fat (g) 1.2
Cholesterol (mg) 0
Sodium (mg) 254
Potassium (mg) 378
Vitamin C (mg) 9

In a large nonstick skillet over medium heat, combine shallots, celery, yellow onions, green onions, garlic, kasha and dill. Cook for 5 minutes, stirring constantly, until vegetables soften. Add broth. Reduce heat and simmer for 20 minutes, or until liquid is absorbed. Remove from heat and set aside. In a large serving bowl, whisk together mustard, wine, garlic powder and lemon zest. Fluff cooked kasha with a fork and spoon into dressing. Mix well with a rubber spatula. When ready to serve, add additional chopped dill.

MAKES 6 SERVINGS

BALSAMIC BAKED ONIONS

Maui, Vidalia or Walla Walla onions become ambrosial when slowly baked with balsamic vinegar. The heavenly flavor is magnified by the addition of fresh rosemary. Serve with grilled or roasted entrées.

fat-free cooking spray

4 sprigs fresh rosemary

4 medium-sized Maui onions,
   peeled

¼ cup balsamic vinegar

2 tablespoons fresh rosemary,
   chopped

MAKES 4 SERVINGS

nutritional
analysis
per serving

Calories (kcal) 59.1
Total Fat (g) 0.7
Cholesterol (mg) 0
Sodium (mg) 25
Potassium (mg) 451
Vitamin C (mg) 30

Preheat oven to 350°. Spray an 8 x 8 baking pan with fat-free cooking spray. Place rosemary sprigs in a baking pan. Cut a thin slice from both ends of onions. Place onions in a pan on top of rosemary. Spray onions with fat-free cooking spray. Drizzle each onion with 2 teaspoons of the vinegar and top with 1 tablespoon of the rosemary. Cover lightly with foil and bake until tender, about 1 hour. Remove foil and spray again with fat-free cooking spray. Divide the remaining 2 tablespoons vinegar and remaining 1 tablespoon rosemary over onions. Return to the oven and bake until onions begin to brown around the edges, about 30 minutes. Serve hot or at room temperature.

main
dishes

MAIN DISHES

fish & seafood	Crab Marinara
	Grilled Salmon with Mango Salsa
	Lemon Pepper Salmon
	Oven-Roasted Mackerel
	Roasted Shad with Herbs
	Seared Tuna with Ginger
	Trout in Parchment
poultry	Chicken Breasts with Vermouth and Capers
	Crispy Dijon Chicken
	Lemon-Marjoram Roasted Chicken
meats	Grilled Herb-Crusted Flank Steak
	Middle Eastern Burgers

THE MAIN MEAL of the day has always been the most important. Even though starting the day with a healthful breakfast is the secret to good health, we tend to place more emphasis on the evening meal. Perhaps it provides us with the opportunity to commune with family and friends or relax after a stressful day.

Learn how to prepare healthful foods in a delicious way. The fish and seafood, meats, game, poultry and vegetarian entrées utilize foods that are naturally low in fat and cholesterol, high in vitamins, minerals and fiber. You can successfully control fat levels, high blood pressure and blood clots, while also enjoying the pleasure of dining.

CRAB MARINARA

Surimi or imitation crab gives this low-fat, low-salt pasta entrée the flavor of the sea.

2 tablespoons clam juice

4 cloves garlic, minced

1 can (28 ounces) crushed low-sodium tomatoes in puree

1 can (8 ounces) low-sodium tomato sauce

1 tablespoon concentrated tomato paste, use tube

½ teaspoon crushed red pepper flakes

1 teaspoon anchovy paste, use tube

2 cups water

1 pound surimi or imitation crab meat

¼ cup cut fresh basil leaves, in thin slices

1 pound penne pasta

nutritional analysis per serving

Calories (kcal) 605.6
Total Fat (g) 3.7
Cholesterol (mg) 34
Sodium (mg) 546
Potassium (mg) 1054
Vitamin C (mg) 42

Heat clam juice over medium-low heat in a large and deep sauté pan. Add garlic and cook for 2 minutes, or until fragrant. Add tomatoes, tomato sauce and paste, red pepper flakes, anchovy paste and water. Bring to a boil. Lower heat to medium-low and simmer briskly for 15 to 20 minutes, or until sauce thickens. Stir in surimi and basil. Cover and set aside. Cook penne according to package directions. Drain and arrange on 4 serving plates. Top with sumiri and marinara sauce.

MAKES 4 SERVINGS

GRILLED SALMON WITH MANGO SALSA

Spice up salmon steaks with south of the boarder seasoning. Cumin, coriander and fresh thyme provide the rub, which is patted on to form a marinade. Mildly hot mango salsa adds a refreshing tangy taste to fresh salmon.

fat-free cooking spray

4 salmon steaks, about 6 ounces each

2½ teaspoons ground cumin

2 teaspoons ground coriander

2 tablespoons fresh thyme

salt and pepper to taste

1 medium mango, chopped

¼ cup chopped pineapple

½ cup diced jícama

1 fresh jalepeño pepper, seeded, stemmed and chopped

2 green onions, white part only, chopped

¼ cup thinly sliced red onion

2 tablespoons fresh lime juice

2 tablespoons fresh orange juice

1 tablespoon fresh lemon juice

¼ cup chopped fresh cilantro

nutritional analysis per serving	
Calories (kcal)	289.9
Total Fat (g)	6.7
Cholesterol (mg)	88
Sodium (mg)	167
Potassium (mg)	1028
Vitamin C (mg)	73

Spray grill with fat-free cooking spray and heat to medium high. Lightly spray salmon steaks with fat-free cooking spray. Mix together cumin, coriander, thyme, salt and pepper. Spread mixture evenly on each steak. Marinate for 10 minutes. In a deep serving bowl, mix together mango, pineapple, jícama, jalapeño pepper, green and red onions, fruit juices and 3 tablespoons of the cilantro. Top salsa with remaining 1 tablespoon cilantro. Chill. Grill salmon for 5 minutes per side, or until fish flakes easily. Serve salmon and pass chilled salsa.

MAKES 4 SERVINGS

LEMON PEPPER SALMON

Salmon fillets marinated in lemon pepper and lemon juice cook nicely indoors under the broiler or outdoors over the grill. An herbed lemon-yogurt dressing echoes the lemony nuances of the fish. Serve with baked potatoes and broccoli spears for a colorful balance to this family-style dinner.

2 cups nonfat plain yogurt

1 tablespoon lemon juice

zest of 1 lemon, grated

2 tablespoons chopped fresh
   oregano

1 tablespoon chopped capers

1 clove garlic, minced

1½ pounds salmon fillets

fat-free cooking spray

lemon pepper to taste

juice of ½ lemon

lemon slices and fresh
oregano sprigs for garnish

MAKES 4 SERVINGS

nutritional analysis per serving	
Calories (kcal)	269.4
Total Fat (g)	6.3
Cholesterol (mg)	91
Sodium (mg)	237
Potassium (mg)	882
Vitamin C (mg)	8

Drain yogurt by placing in a sieve over a deep bowl. Cover and refrigerate overnight. Remove yogurt from sieve and place in a small serving bowl, discarding liquid from yogurt. Add lemon juice, zest, oregano, capers and garlic. Mix well and refrigerate.

Preheat broiler. Wash and dry salmon. Place rack on a foil-lined baking sheet and spray with fat-free cooking spray. Arrange fillets on a rack. Sprinkle evenly with lemon pepper and moisten with lemon juice. Marinate for 10 minutes. Spray fillets lightly with fat-free cooking spray. Broil for 6 minutes, or until fish flakes easily but is still moist. Remove to a platter and garnish with lemon slices and oregano sprigs. Serve with yogurt dressing.

Oven-Roasted Mackerel

A simple combination of garlic, herbs, breadcrumbs and clam juice enhances the savory flavor of mackerel. If you can't locate this fish at your local supermarket, try Asian food stores.

2 small whole mackerel, about 1 pound each
fat-free cooking spray
4 cloves garlic, minced
¼ cup chopped fresh flat-leaf parsley
2 teaspoons chopped fresh oregano
2 tablespoons grated pecorino romano cheese
¾ cup breadcrumbs
2 tablespoons clam juice
4 fresh oregano sprigs for garnish
4 lemon wedges for garnish

MAKES 4 SERVINGS

nutritional analysis per serving

Calories (kcal)	340.8
Total Fat (g)	6.7
Cholesterol (mg)	122
Sodium (mg)	549
Potassium (mg)	1055
Vitamin C (mg)	10

Preheat oven to 400°. Line a baking sheet with parchment paper. (Foil may be used, but must be sprayed with a fat-free cooking spray so fish does not stick.) Cut off and discard head and tail. Slit fish on belly side, remove viscera and open flat. Run a sharp knife along the backbone from the top down to the tail. Place a knife along the backbone, under the bones, cutting outward toward the ends. Do so on both sides so the spine can be removed and discarded. Cut each fish down the middle into 2 fillets. Place prepared fillets skin side down on the baking sheet. Set aside. Combine garlic, parsley, oregano, cheese, breadcrumbs and clam juice. Mix well. Spoon dressing evenly over fillets. Bake until dressing is brown and fish flakes easily when pierced with a fork, about 8 to 10 minutes. Cut into 4 portions, place on a platter and garnish with fresh oregano and lemon wedges. Serve immediately.

Roasted Shad with Herbs

The American shad, a cold saltwater fish, is a member of the herring family and usually available in the spring. Cut seasonal vegetables. Dust vegetables with herbs and roast at the same time you're grilling the fish.

fat-free cooking spray

1 whole dressed shad, about
   3 to 4 pounds

4 cloves garlic, thinly sliced

1 small onion, thinly sliced

2 medium lemons, sliced

1 tomato, thinly sliced

6 sprigs fresh tarragon

6 sprigs fresh marjoram

6 sprigs fresh thyme

6 sprigs fresh mint

4 bay leaves

lemon wedges and fresh mint
   sprigs for garnish

nutritional analysis per serving	
Calories (kcal)	751.8
Total Fat (g)	48.6
Cholesterol (mg)	255
Sodium (mg)	326
Potassium (mg)	1829
Vitamin C (mg)	53

Preheat oven to 450°. Lightly spray a baking sheet with fat-free cooking spray. Arrange fish on a baking sheet. Place half amounts of garlic, onion, lemon, tomato, tarragon, marjoram, thyme, mint and bay leaves inside fish's cavity. Strew other half of garlic, onion, lemon and tomato and herbs over fish. Roast fish for 25 to 30 minutes, or until skin is crisp and flesh cooked through. Garnish with lemon wedges and mint sprigs. Cool for 5 minutes before serving.

Makes 4 servings

SEARED TUNA WITH GINGER

This quick-to-prepare tuna has Japanese flavors. Mirin, Japanese sweet cooking wine, is available at Asian markets and lends a distinctive flavor to the mildly seasoned sauce. Serve with short-grained and somewhat sticky sushi rice. Flavor with rice vinegar and top with snipped sheets of nori.

1 tablespoon rice vinegar

1 tablespoon grated
   fresh ginger

3 tablespoons mirin

3 tablespoons low-sodium
   soy sauce

4 ahi tuna steaks, about
   1½ inches thick and 6
   ounces each

2 green onions, finely
   chopped

MAKES 4 SERVINGS

nutritional analysis per serving	
Calories (kcal)	294.9
Total Fat (g)	8.6
Cholesterol (mg)	65
Sodium (mg)	442
Potassium (mg)	681
Vitamin C (mg)	14

In a small saucepan, add rice vinegar, ginger, 2 tablespoons of the mirin and 2 tablespoons of the soy sauce. Heat over low heat, stirring constantly until warm. Set aside. Combine remaining 1 tablespoon mirin, 1 tablespoon soy sauce and rub over tuna. In a large nonstick skillet, cook tuna over high heat for 1 minute per side for medium-rare, or until done. Remove tuna from pan, sprinkle with green onions and serve with remaining mirin sauce.

NOTE Place seared tuna in a preheated oven at 350° for several minutes for medium-well done.

TROUT IN PARCHMENT

Fresh water trout is baked on a bed of celery greens, onions, lemon and dill. These delicate seasonings complement the fish's mild flavor, and the parchment paper allows the flavoring to permeate the flesh and keep it moist.

4 trout fillets

4 tablespoons grated lemon zest

2 teaspoons freshly ground pepper

3¼ cups chopped celery greens

3¼ cups fresh dill

1 large onion, sliced into thin rings

1 lemon, thinly sliced

4 tablespoons Chablis

4 sheets parchment paper

MAKES 4 SERVINGS

nutritional analysis per serving

Calories (kcal) 248.7
Total Fat (g) 7.3
Cholesterol (mg) 46
Sodium (mg) 290
Potassium (mg) 1817
Vitamin C (mg) 33

Preheat oven to 400°. Place parchment sheets on a working surface. Wash, dry and sprinkle each fillet with 1 tablespoon of the lemon zest and ½ teaspoon of the ground pepper. Set aside. Make a bed for each fillet by stacking half of the celery greens, dill, onion and lemon slices in the center of each parchment sheet. Place 1 seasoned trout fillet on each bed. Cover with remaining celery greens, dill, onion and lemon slices. Drizzle 1 tablespoon of the Chablis over each fillet. Quickly seal packets by covering the fillets with the bottom third of the parchment sheet, fold sides toward middle and roll up toward the top. Tuck the end under the packet. Place the packets on a baking sheet. Bake until fish is fragrant and cooked through, about 13 to 15 minutes. Immediately serve in the packets so each diner can open and enjoy the aroma.

CHICKEN BREASTS WITH VERMOUTH AND CAPERS

Soy milk is the ingredient that adds richness without fat to the chicken breasts. Make a day ahead or in the morning to allow flavors to marinate. The tang of lemon zest and the crunch of dry-roasted soy nuts accent this unusual presentation. Nutty brown basmati rice adds fiber and provides a flavorful side dish.

MARINADE

½ cup lemon juice

1 cup dry vermouth

4 cloves garlic, minced

1½ teaspoons dried oregano

4 boneless chicken breasts, halved

fat-free cooking spray

1 clove garlic, minced

4 cups broccoli spears, cut diagonally

1 cup defatted low-sodium chicken broth

2 tablespoons rinsed, drained tiny capers

1 tablespoon cornstarch

¼ cup soy milk

2 tablespoons grated lemon zest for garnish

1 cup unsalted dry-roasted soy nuts for garnish

MAKES 4 SERVINGS

nutritional analysis per serving	
Calories (kcal)	578.4
Total Fat (g)	25.0
Cholesterol (mg)	93
Sodium (mg)	367
Potassium (mg)	1388
Vitamin C (mg)	104
Vitamin E	

In a 2-cup glass measuring pitcher, combine lemon juice, vermouth, garlic and oregano. Mix well and pour into a large freezer bag. Set aside. Slice each chicken breast across the grain into ½-inch slices and place in marinade. Seal bag, fold over so chicken is under marinade and place in the refrigerator to marinate for 6 to 8 hours. Remove chicken pieces from marinade. Discard marinade.

Lightly spray a large nonstick skillet or electric frying pan with fat-free cooking spray. Stir-fry chicken over medium-high heat and partially cook for 2 minutes. Remove chicken from pan and keep warm. Add garlic and broccoli to pan and stir-fry until crisp-tender. Return chicken and accumulated juices to pan. Add chicken broth and capers. Cover and cook over medium-low heat for 3 minutes, or until broccoli softens and chicken is cooked through. Mix cornstarch with soy milk and stir into chicken-broccoli mixture until liquid thickens. Place on a serving dish and garnish with lemon zest and soy nuts.

NOTE   A rice cooker is a good investment for faster cooking and easier cleanup. Most rice cookers can also be used as steamers and food warmers.

CRISPY DIJON CHICKEN

Oven-fried chicken takes on a hot and spicy personality with the addition of Dijon mustard and cayenne pepper. Grape Nuts cereal supplies the crunch and fiber. Serve with garlic mashed potatoes and lemony green beans for a nutritious, quick to prepare dinner.

fat free cooking spray

¼ cup Dijon mustard

juice of 1 lemon

1½ cups Grape Nuts cereal, crushed

1 tablespoon paprika

2 tablespoons dried tarragon

3 pounds chicken parts, skinned

MAKES 4 SERVINGS

nutritional analysis per serving

Calories (kcal) 610.87
Total Fat (g) 19.2
Cholesterol (mg) 186
Sodium (mg) 666
Potassium (mg) 796
Vitamin C (mg) 6

Preheat oven to 400°. Lightly spray a foil-lined baking sheet with fat-free cooking spray. Set aside. Whisk together mustard and lemon juice. Set aside. In a heavy plastic bag, mix together Grape Nuts, paprika and tarragon. Roll chicken pieces in mustard mixture. Shake in Grape Nuts mixture until well coated. Place chicken on a rack to dry. When all pieces are coated, place them on a foil-lined baking sheet. Bake until chicken is brown and crunchy, about 30 to 35 minutes.

LEMON-MARJORAM ROASTED CHICKEN

A fat free citrus-herb mixture placed under the skin, gives this chicken its zesty flavor.

1 chicken, about 3 pounds,
  cut into bite-sized pieces

¾ cup lemon juice

1 cup white wine

2 cloves garlic, crushed

zest of 1 lemon

2 (4 inch) sprigs fresh
  marjoram

salt and pepper to taste

4 tablespoons minced lemon
  rind

4 tablespoons chopped fresh
  marjoram leaves

2 tablespoons chopped green
  onion

fat-free cooking spray

nutritional
analysis
per serving

Calories (kcal) 491.5
Total Fat (g) 18.2
Cholesterol (mg) 186
Sodium (mg) 219
Potassium (mg) 661
Vitamin C (mg) 33

Wash chicken pieces and place into a large plastic bag. Pour in lemon juice and wine. Add garlic, lemon peel, marjoram, salt and pepper. Seal and refrigerate for at least 6 hours. Remove chicken pieces from marinade and wipe chicken with a paper towel. Gently loosen skin. Combine lemon rind, marjoram and green onion, and place about a spoonful under the skin of each chicken piece. Preheat oven to 400°. Lightly spray a foil-covered baking sheet with fat free cooking spray. Place chicken pieces on prepared baking sheet. Place on center rack of oven, and roast until skin is crisp and chicken is cooked, about 35 minutes.

MAKES 4 SERVINGS

GRILLED HERB-CRUSTED FLANK STEAK

Dijon mustard and red wine tenderize the steak, while the dried herbs and peppercorns provide the crust for this special treat. Take care not to overcook, since this lean cut of beef dries out fast.

¼ cup Dijon mustard

2 tablespoons red table wine

1½ pounds flank steak

2 tablespoons dried marjoram

1½ tablespoons dried thyme

1½ tablespoons dried oregano

coarsely ground black peppercorns

MAKES 6 SERVINGS

nutritional
analysis
per serving

Calories (kcal) 224.6
Total Fat (g) 12.6
Cholesterol (mg) 58
Sodium (mg) 207
Potassium (mg) 471
Vitamin C (mg) 0

Make a paste with the mustard and wine. Rub on flank steak. Place in a plastic bag and refrigerate for 8 to 10 hours. Remove from bag and wipe beef dry with paper towels. Mix herbs and peppercorns together and rub into steak. Grill for 4 to 6 minutes per side, or until desired degree of doneness. Slice across grain and serve.

Middle Eastern Burgers

Mixing lean ground round steak with tofu reduces the fat and increases the protein. The grilled vegetables and yogurt sauce help to give this dish its exotic flavor.

fat-free cooking spray or extra
　　virgin fat free cooking spray

1 cups nonfat plain yogurt

3 tablespoons chopped fresh
　　mint leaves

3 tablespoons minced garlic

1 ½ teaspoons salt

¾ teaspoon crushed red
　　pepper flakes

1 teaspoon cinnamon

1 teaspoon paprika

½ teaspoon allspice

1 large onion, cut into 1-inch
　　slices

½ large red onion, cut into
　　¼-inch slices

3 medium tomatoes, cut into
　　1-inch rounds

¼ cup chopped fresh cilantro
　　leaves

1 pound round steak, fat
　　removed, ground twice

1 cup firm tofu

1 small bunch spinach leaves

8 pita breads

Makes 4 servings

nutritional analysis per serving	
Calories (kcal) 702.3	
Total Fat (g) 20.3	
Cholesterol (mg) 68	
Sodium (mg) 1712	
Potassium (mg) 1228	
Vitamin C (mg) 36	
Vitamin E	

Preheat oven to 400° and prepare barbecue for grilling. Spray a large baking sheet with fat-free cooking spray. Mix together yogurt, mint and 1 tablespoon of the garlic. Set aside. Mix together salt, red pepper flakes, cinnamon, paprika and allspice. Set aside. Arrange onions and tomatoes on prepared baking sheet. Sprinkle ½ of the spice mixture, cilantro and 1 tablespoon of the garlic over vegetables. Bake until vegetables are brown around edges, about 20 minutes. Place vegetables in a serving bowl and keep warm.

Drain tofu of water. Place in a clean kitchen towel, twist both ends to secure tofu and gently knead to remove as much water as possible. Tofu should look like dry cottage cheese. Place squeezed tofu into a medium bowl, add steak, remaining 1 tablespoon of garlic and remaining half of spice mixture. Mix well and shape into 4 patties. Grill patties 4 to 6 inches above coals for 12 minutes for medium-well done, turning once. Place spinach leaves on a serving platter. Toast pita breads around edge of grill during the last 2 minutes of cooking. Arrange burgers on spinach leaves and garnish with roasted vegetables. Serve with reserved yogurt sauce and toasted pita breads.

OSTRICH GRILLED ARGENTINE-STYLE

Ostrich tenderloin is marinated in a tangy, garlicky chimichurri-style parsley sauce and quickly grilled. Serve steaks with a simple green salad, plenty of crusty bread and a robust Argentine red wine.

1 pound ostrich tenderloin

salt and white pepper to taste

2 cups fresh flat-leaf parsley, packed

1 cup fat-free Italian dressing

2 tablespoons water

5 cloves garlic, crushed

several grindings of black pepper

fat-free cooking spray

MAKES 4 SERVINGS

nutritional analysis per serving

Calories (kcal)	197
Total Fat (g)	3.7
Cholesterol (mg)	96.3
Sodium (mg)	891
Potassium (mg)	202
Vitamin C (mg)	41

Cut ostrich tenderloin into 4 flat steaks. Salt, pepper and place steaks in a stainless steel baking pan. Set aside. Pulse parsley, dressing, water, garlic and black pepper with a food processor. Pulse until sauce becomes thick and shiny, about 40 seconds. Pour half of the sauce into a small serving bowl and set aside. Pour remaining sauce over steaks. Cover and marinate in the refrigerator for 30 minutes, turning every 10 minutes. Spray grill with fat-free cooking spray and preheat. When coals are white, remove steaks from marinade, drain and place on hot grill. Cook for 4 or 5 minutes on each side, or until rare or medium-rare. Remove from grill and serve with remaining chimichurri sauce.

SWEET AND SOUR RABBIT

Rabbit is enjoying a resurgence of popularity on restaurant menus. Lower in fat and cholesterol than most meat, it is a good choice for healthful dining. The flavorful herb-infused wine marinade brings out the taste without the extra fat.

1½ cups dry white wine

1½ cups water

1 large onion, thinly sliced

2 cloves garlic, minced

1 bouquet garni of fresh
    rosemary, sage and fennel
    sprigs

1 bay leaf

1 teaspoon sea salt

1 teaspoon freshly ground
    pepper

2½ to 3 pounds rabbit pieces

flour to coat

fat-free cooking spray

2 tablespoons each white
    wine vinegar and sugar,
    mixed together

½ cup dry-cured pitted
    black olives

fresh flat-leaf parsley for
    garnish

nutritional analysis per serving

Calories (kcal)	559.0
Total Fat (g)	18.1
Cholesterol (mg)	162
Sodium (mg)	900
Potassium (mg)	1279
Vitamin C (mg)	8

In a large saucepan, combine wine, water, onion, garlic, bouquet of garni, bay leaf, salt and pepper. Bring to a boil. Remove from heat and cool. In a large plastic bag, combine rabbit pieces and cooled marinade. Seal shut and refrigerate for 4 hours or overnight. Remove rabbit pieces from marinade and set aside. Bring marinade to a boil over high heat, strain and set aside. Wipe rabbit pieces dry and lightly coat with flour. Heat a large nonstick skillet sprayed with fat-free cooking spray. Add half of the rabbit pieces and cook for 5 minutes on each side, or until well browned. Remove and keep warm. Repeat procedure with remaining rabbit pieces. Pour marinade into a skillet and add vinegar with sugar. Bring to a boil, scraping up brown bits. Return reserved rabbit and accumulated juices to skillet, lower heat and cover. Simmer for 30 minutes, or until rabbit is cooked through. Remove rabbit from skillet and place with olives on a serving platter. Keep warm. Reduce sauce to high heat until thickened. Pour over rabbit and olives. Garnish with parsley and serve immediately.

MAKES 4 SERVINGS

Turkey Scaloppine

A variation on veal piccata, low-fat turkey stars with fresh mushrooms, capers, orange and lemon zest. The addition of tarragon and sherry vinegar gives this Italian dish a sophisticated continental flavor.

fat-free cooking spray

2 cups sliced mushrooms caps

1 teaspoon garlic powder

1½ pounds turkey breast slices, pounded very thin flour to coat

salt and freshly ground pepper to taste

¼ cup chopped fresh tarragon

¼ cup all-purpose flour

⅔ cup dry Marsala wine

1 tablespoon sherry vinegar

1 cup defatted low-sodium beef broth

2 tablespoons rinsed dried small capers

2 tablespoons grated orange zest

1 teaspoon grated lemon zest

additional fresh tarragon sprigs for garnish

orange wedges for garnish

nutritional analysis per serving

Calories (kcal) 232.5
Total Fat (g) 7.5
Cholesterol (mg) 66
Sodium (mg) 294
Potassium (mg) 438
Vitamin C (mg) 3

In a large nonstick skillet sprayed with fat-free cooking spray, sauté mushrooms with a pinch of garlic powder over high heat. Stir constantly for 4 minutes, or until cooked. Remove mushrooms to a warm bowl and set aside. Lightly coat turkey slices with flour and season with salt, pepper and several pinches of garlic powder and tarragon. In the same skillet, cook turkey slices in one layer for 4 minutes, or until brown, turning once. Arrange slices in a 6 x 9 baking dish and keep warm.

Preheat oven to 350°. Add flour and Marsala to skillet. Whisk together until smooth. Add vinegar, broth, capers and orange and lemon zests. Cook on high heat for 2 minutes, or until gravy thickens, stirring constantly. Sprinkle mushrooms over turkey slices and pour sauce to cover. Sprinkle top with remaining tarragon. Cover and bake until brown and bubbly, about 40 minutes. Remove from oven and serve garnished with tarragon sprigs and orange wedges.

Makes 6 servings

PHEASANT TARRAGON

Farm-raised pheasant is available at specialty food markets and tends to be more flavorful than wild pheasant. These birds are lean and appear to have more flesh than their country cousins. Prepare this dish with the *Pheasant Broth*, page 169, a day or two in advance so the birds can marinate.

2 pheasants, cut into 8 serving
   pieces, reserved backs and
   necks for *Pheasant Broth*
salt and pepper to taste
dried tarragon to taste
fat-free cooking spray
4 cups plus 2 tablespoons
   Pheasant Broth, page169,
   or defatted low-sodium
   chicken broth
3 cloves garlic, thinly sliced
1 cup button mushrooms
1 cup cognac or brandy
2 tablespoons Dijon mustard
1½ cups white wine
2 tablespoons all-purpose flour
carrots from *Pheasant Broth*,
   page 169, or 4 medium
   carrots, cooked
1 cup frozen white onions,
   thawed
chopped fresh flat-leaf parsley
   for garnish
chopped fresh tarragon for
   garnish
soft polenta, optional

nutritional
analysis
per serving
(without polenta)

Calories (kcal)	666.3
Total Fat (g)	25.1
Cholesterol (mg)	189
Sodium (mg)	609
Potassium (mg)	1013
Vitamin C (mg)	21

Salt, pepper and rub pheasant pieces with tarragon. In a deep non-stick skillet sprayed with fat-free cooking spray, sauté pheasant in batches over medium heat, until deep brown. Remove and keep warm. Lower heat and in the same skillet add 2 tablespoons of the *Pheasant Broth*. Add garlic and mushrooms and cook until fragrant. Pour cognac into skillet. Raise heat and bring to a boil. Lower heat to medium. Return pheasant to skillet. Whisk together mustard and wine and pour over pheasant. Whisk together flour and ½ cup of the *Pheasant Broth* and stir into skillet. Gradually add remaining 3½ cups broth, covering pheasant with broth. Turn heat down to a simmer and cook for 1 hour. Add cooked carrots and onions. Continue to simmer for 30 minutes, or until pheasant is tender. Taste and adjust seasoning. Garnish with parsley and fresh tarragon. Prepare polenta from package instructions and serve with pheasant, if desired.

MAKES 6 SERVINGS

PHEASANT BROTH

Use this recipe with *Pheasant Tarragon*, page 168. For easy preparation, freeze pheasant parts or roasted carcasses to have on hand when making this broth.

backs and necks of at least 2
    pheasants
2 onions, or 4 shallots, halved
4 cloves garlic
4 medium carrots
2 stalks celery
dash of mixed fresh herbs,
    basil, thyme, rosemary,
    oregano or parsley
salt and pepper to taste

MAKES 3 QUARTS

nutritional
analysis
per serving
(1 cup)

Calories (kcal) 79.9
Total Fat (g) 5.7
Cholesterol (mg) 16
Sodium (mg) 128
Potassium (mg) 155
Vitamin C (mg) 4

Preheat oven to 500°. In a shallow Dutch oven, roast pheasant bones for 20 minutes, or until deep brown. Remove from oven and add onions, garlic, carrots, celery, herbs, salt and pepper. Cover with water and bring to a boil. Lower heat, cover and simmer gently for 2 hours, or until vegetables are cooked and broth is savory. Strain broth, discarding bones and vegetables, except carrots. Rub skin from carrots and reserve for *Pheasant Tarragon*. Broth can be stored in 2-cup containers in the freezer for several months.

Baked-Stuffed Mexican Peppers

Try a different variation of chiles rellenos. This lighter preparation method cuts fat without sacrificing flavor. Serve with steamed rice, black beans and fresh corn.

fat-free cooking spray

1 pound Anaheim peppers or long sweet Italian peppers

1 package (8 ounces) low-fat Neufchâtel cheese

1 dash hot sauce

1 cup bay shrimp

¾ cup finely chopped almonds

⅓ cup chopped fresh cilantro

2 egg whites

1 tablespoon water

½ cup all-purpose flour

¼ teaspoon sage

1 pinch dried oregano

flour to coat

2 fresh cilantro sprigs for garnish

Makes 6 servings

nutritional analysis per serving

Calories (kcal) 359.0
Total Fat (g) 19.2
Cholesterol (mg) 89
Sodium (mg) 237
Potassium (mg) 585
Vitamin C (mg) 190
Vitamin E

Preheat oven to 400°. Lightly spray an 11 x 14 baking sheet with fat-free cooking spray and set aside. Wash and dry peppers. Place peppers directly under broiler until skin blisters on all sides, or singe over a gas flame. Skin immediately, and slit and remove seeds and membrane. Set aside. Whip together cheese with hot sauce. Fold in shrimp, ½ cup of the almonds and cilantro. Mix well and set aside. In a shallow dish, whip together egg whites and water. In a second shallow dish, combine flour with sage and oregano. Stuff each pepper with a portion of shrimp mixture, coat with egg white mixture, roll in flour and dip again into egg white mixture. Place on prepared baking sheet. Sprinkle coated peppers with remaining ¼ cup almonds. Bake until peppers are golden brown, about 25 minutes. Remove from oven, garnish with cilantro sprigs and serve immediately.

LENTILS AND RICE

Prepare a classic Indian dish with red and brown lentils, basmati rice and a touch of curry. To keep the textures and colors true, precook lentils in separate pots.

1 cup brown lentils

1 cup red lentils

4 cups water

½ teaspoon crushed red pepper flakes

½ teaspoon cumin seeds

3 teaspoons curry powder

1 teaspoon ground coriander

¼ cup low-sodium vegetable broth

1½ cups chopped celery

1 medium onion, finely chopped

4 cups cooked basmati rice

½ cup finely chopped fresh cilantro

½ cup finely chopped red onion

1 head kale, steamed, for garnish

½ small red onion, sliced into thin rings

¼ cup chopped fresh cilantro

tomato and lime wedges for garnish

nutritional analysis per serving	
Calories (kcal)	707.3
Total Fat (g)	1.7
Cholesterol (mg)	0
Sodium (mg)	162
Potassium (mg)	910
Vitamin C (mg)	35

Wash and pick over lentils, discarding debris. In 2 separate 2-quart pans, place lentils according to color. Pour 2 cups of the water in each pan, cover and bring to a boil. Lower heat and simmer red lentils for 8 minutes and brown lentils for 18 minutes, or until most of the liquid has been absorbed. Set aside. In a large nonstick sauté pan, cook red pepper flakes, cumin seeds, curry powder and coriander until aromatic, stirring constantly. Lower heat and add broth, celery and onions. Cover and cook for 10 minutes, or until onions are soft and celery is tender. Fold in lentils, rice, fresh coriander and red onion. Mix well. Place on a kale-lined serving platter. Top with onion rings and cilantro leaves. Garnish platter with tomato and lime wedges.

MAKES 6 SERVINGS

SPAGHETTI SQUASH WITH PASTA

Spaghetti squash is a pale yellow, watermelon-shaped squash. When cooked, the flesh of the squash separates into spaghetti-like strands from its rind. The mild-tasting flesh works well with seasoned sauces or herbal treatments. Serve with a tomato-basil salad and sourdough bread for a light vegetarian dinner.

1 medium spaghetti squash,
    about 6 pounds
½ pound ridged penne pasta
2 medium onions, thinly sliced
2 tablespoons chopped fresh
    sage
1 tablespoon fresh thyme
¼ pound Gorgonzola cheese,
    crumbled
salt and pepper to taste
1 tablespoon white truffle oil,
    optional

MAKES 4 SERVINGS

nutritional
analysis
per serving

Calories (kcal) 553.2
Total Fat (g) 13.2
Cholesterol (mg) 21
Sodium (mg) 824
Potassium (mg) 994
Vitamin C (mg) 18

Preheat oven to 350°. With a fork, prick squash all over and place on a foil-lined baking sheet. Bake, turning once, until squash yields to the touch, about 1½ hours. Set aside. Cook pasta according to package directions. Drain and keep warm. In a large round microwave-safe dish, add onion and cover bowl with plastic wrap. Cook on full power for 10 minutes, or until translucent, turning once. Remove cover, add sage and thyme. Cut squash in half lengthwise. Remove seeds and fibers from squash. With a fork, lift out spaghetti-like strands and add to onion mixture. Mix well. Fold in cheese and pasta. Add salt, pepper and white truffle oil, if desired. Serve immediately.

desserts

DESSERTS

cakes	Vanilla-Nut Cake with Rum Glaze
	Kahlúa Chocolate Angel Food Cake
	Tropical Spice Cake
	Chocolate Fudge Cake
pies	French Apple Crumb Pie
	Fresh Apricot and Blueberry Pie
puddings	Puddings
	Old-Fashioned Brown Rice Pudding
	Tofu Bread Pudding
cookies & other treats	Hazelnut Macaroons
	Baklava
	Biscotti
	Cherries Flambé with Frozen Yogurt

DESSERTS

For most people, dinner is not complete without a dessert, and for most of us that means something sweet. Fresh fruit or fruit-based desserts are the most healthful choices because they are naturally sweet. Enjoy puddings, cakes, pies and frozen desserts by choosing ingredients that are low in fat and cholesterol.

When purchasing prepared desserts, read labels carefully to determine fat content. When preparing desserts at home, try using these fat substitutes: fruit purees and nectars, nonfat milk, low-fat soy milk, honey, molasses, corn syrup, jams, grated raw or mashed cooked carrots, sweet potatoes and squash, flaxseed meal and lecithin granules. Increase the nutritional value of desserts by using whole grain flours and unrefined sweeteners.

Some of the desserts that follow are variations on themes, like baklava or angel food cake. The low-fat recipes tend to make biscotti crispier, puddings creamier and cakes more rustic. With these recipes, you'll learn how to prepare good healthful desserts for your family and friends.

VANILLA-NUT CAKE WITH RUM GLAZE

This elegant cake owes its texture and rise to lecithin, which is a by-product from soy bean oil refining. It is a nutritious way to soften the texture and lesson the density of low-fat breads and cakes. It is available at health food stores in the bulk bins. Refrigerate lecithin granules to retain freshness.

fat-free cooking spray

2½ cups all-purpose flour

¾ cup oat bran

1¼ cups sugar

1 tablespoon lecithin granules

2 teaspoons baking powder

2 tablespoons applesauce

1¾ cups nonfat milk

2 egg whites, beaten

2 teaspoons vanilla extract

¼ cup plus 2 tablespoons finely chopped toasted walnuts

½ cup confectioners' sugar

1½ tablespoons dark rum

MAKES 8 SERVINGS

nutritional analysis per serving	
Calories (kcal)	401.9
Total Fat (g)	6.4
Cholesterol (mg)	1
Sodium (mg)	134
Potassium (mg)	232
Vitamin C (mg)	1
Vitamin E	

Preheat oven to 350°. Lightly spray an 8-cup Bundt pan with fat-free cooking spray. Set aside. In a large bowl, mix together flour, oat bran, sugar, lecithin granules and baking powder. Add applesauce, milk, egg whites and vanilla. Stir until ingredients are well mixed. Fold in ¼ cup of the walnuts. Spread in prepared pan. Bake until a toothpick inserted in the center comes out clean, about 40 to 45 minutes. Remove cake from oven and cool in the pan for 20 minutes. Invert onto a wire rack to cool completely. Whisk together confectioners' sugar and rum. Drizzle over cake and sprinkle with remaining 2 tablespoons walnuts. Serve warm.

KAHLÚA CHOCOLATE ANGEL FOOD CAKE

Far from the cottony taste of commercially prepared angel food cake, the intriguing flavors of coffee and chocolate blend with the vanilla and cinnamon seasoning in this unusual cake. Enjoy a slice with a cup of chicory-blended coffee for a taste of old New Orleans.

¾ cup sifted cake flour

1 ¼ cups sugar

⅓ cup unsweetened Dutch processed cocoa powder

1 ¼ teaspoons cinnamon

8 large egg whites, room temperature

1 teaspoon cream of tartar

½ teaspoon vanilla extract

1 teaspoon Kahlúa liqueur

MAKES 12 SERVINGS

nutritional analysis per serving

Calories (kcal) 125.0
Total Fat (g) 0.4
Cholesterol (mg) 0
Sodium (mg) 38
Potassium (mg) 118
Vitamin C (mg) 0

Preheat oven to 325º. Sift together flour, sugar, cocoa and cinnamon. Mix well and set aside. In a large electric mixer bowl, beat egg whites at high speed until frothy. Add cream of tartar and beat until egg whites stand in soft peaks. Beat in vanilla and Kahlúa. With a spatula, carefully fold flour mixture into egg whites until mixture is uniform. Spoon batter evenly into an ungreased 10-inch tube pan. Place in the middle of the oven and bake for 50 minutes. Turn off heat and leave cake in oven for an additional 10 minutes. Remove from oven and invert the pan onto a long-necked bottle to cool upside down. When cake is completely cool, remove from pan.

Tropical Spice Cake

Pineapple glaze and chopped Brazil nuts form an elegant topping for this "taste of the islands" spice cake. Flax seed meal, the healthful fat substitute, adds moisture and gives additional nutty flavor. Serve after a light meal, since the cake is rather heavy.

fat-free cooking spray

1 ½ cups all-purpose flour

1 cup whole wheat flour

1 tablespoon plus 1 ½ teaspoons lecithin granules

¾ cup flaxseed meal

1 cup brown sugar, packed

2 teaspoons baking soda

1 teaspoon allspice

½ teaspoon ground cloves

2 teaspoons cinnamon

2 egg whites

1 cup mashed bananas

½ cup nonfat plain yogurt

¼ cup plus 1 teaspoon pineapple juice

⅓ cup crushed drained pineapple

⅓ cup plus 3 tablespoons finely chopped Brazil nuts

½ cup confectioners' sugar

nutritional analysis per serving

Calories (kcal) 294.9
Total Fat (g) 6.6
Cholesterol (mg) 0
Sodium (mg) 236
Potassium (mg) 327
Vitamin C (mg) 5

Preheat oven to 325°. Lightly spray a 12-cup Bundt pan with fat-free cooking spray. Set aside. Mix together flours, lecithin granules, flaxseed meal, brown sugar, baking soda, allspice, cloves and 1 ½ teaspoons of the cinnamon. Set aside. In a large bowl, beat egg whites, bananas, yogurt and ¼ cup of the pineapple juice until well mixed. Fold in flour mixture, pineapple and ⅓ cup of the Brazil nuts. Pour into prepared pan. Bake until a toothpick inserted into cake comes out dry, about 30 minutes. Remove cake from oven and cool in the pan for 20 minutes. Gently remove from pan and cool completely on a wire rack. Whisk together confectioners' sugar with remaining 1 teaspoon pineapple juice and remaining ½ teaspoon cinnamon. Pour over cake. Top with remaining 3 tablespoons Brazil nuts.

Makes 12 servings

CHOCOLATE FUDGE CAKE

This moist, dark chocolate cake conceals the fact that it is made with a little oil and is egg-free. Its flavor is so rich and chocolatey that frosting is not necessary. For a special treat, serve with a scoop of light vanilla ice cream.

fat-free cooking spray

1 ¾ cups all-purpose flour

¾ cup sugar

½ cup Dutch cocoa powder

1 ½ teaspoons baking soda

⅛ teaspoon salt

1 cup low-fat buttermilk

2 tablespoons canola oil

½ cup fig or prune puree

2 teaspoons vanilla extract

MAKES 6 SERVINGS

nutritional analysis per serving

Calories (kcal) 316.4
Total Fat (g) 6.3
Cholesterol (mg) 1
Sodium (mg) 405
Potassium (mg) 249
Vitamin C (mg) 1

Preheat oven to 375°. Lightly spray an 8-inch square baking pan with fat-free cooking spray. Set aside. Combine flour, sugar, cocoa, baking soda and salt. Add buttermilk, oil, prune puree and vanilla. Mix well until smooth. Evenly spread batter into prepared pan. Bake until cake pulls away from sides of pan and is cooked through, about 30 minutes. Cool in pan and serve.

FRENCH APPLE CRUMB PIE

Tart apples combined with plump raisins and walnuts are easy to prepare in this crumb pie. Try it à la mode with low-fat ice cream or nonfat frozen yogurt.

CRUST

fat-free cooking spray

½ cup walnuts

1½ cups Grape Nut Flakes

¼ cup sugar

1 tablespoon cinnamon

2 tablespoons apple juice
   concentrate

1 large egg white

FILLING

6 cups peeled thinly sliced
   apples

½ cup raisins

1 tablespoon all-purpose flour

¾ cup brown sugar, packed

¼ teaspoon salt

1 teaspoon nutmeg

½ teaspoon allspice

¼ cup ground cloves

2 teaspoons cinnamon

MAKES 6 SERVINGS

nutritional analysis per serving	
Calories (kcal)	383.5
Total Fat (g)	8.3
Cholesterol (mg)	0
Sodium (mg)	238
Potassium (mg)	670
Vitamin C (mg)	27

Preheat oven to 350°. Lightly spray a 10-inch pie pan with fat-free cooking spray. Chop walnuts by pulsing with a food processor. Spoon into a medium bowl. Set aside. Pulse Grape Nut Flakes into a course crumb in the food processor. Add to walnuts with sugar, cinnamon, apple juice concentrate and egg white. Mix well. Spoon all but 1 cup of the crumb mixture into prepared pie pan. Press down with a spatula to line pan with crumb mixture. Bake until set, about 8 minutes. Remove from oven and place pan on a rack to cool. Increase oven temperature to 400°. In a large bowl, add apple slices and raisins and coat with flour. Add brown sugar, salt, nutmeg, allspice, cloves and cinnamon. Spoon apple mixture into cooled pie shell and sprinkle with remaining 1 cup crumb mixture, pressing down on crumbs. Bake pie until top is brown and apples are soft, about 40 minutes. If crumb topping seems to brown too fast, cover with foil after 20 minutes, but remove it the last few minutes of baking to recrisp. Cut into 6 wedges to serve.

VARIATION   Try this pie with pears, plums, peaches, apricots, cherries or nectarines in place of the apples.

Fresh Apricot and Blueberry Pie

Sweet, tart, crunchy and creamy best describe this festive fruit pie. Sweet apricots, tart blueberries, crunchy crust and creamy tofu provide the symphony of contrasts. Fill the pie just before serving to maintain its crisp, nutty crust.

3 (12 x 17) phyllo sheets

fat-free cooking spray

¼ cup apricot nectar

3 tablespoons finely chopped toasted almonds

1 packet unflavored gelatin

¼ cup cold water

2 cups silken tofu

1 tablespoon sugar

1 teaspoon almond extract

6 ripe apricots, sliced

1 cup blueberries

¼ cup apricot preserves, warmed in microwave

Makes 8 servings

nutritional analysis per serving	
Calories (kcal)	142.0
Total Fat (g)	4.8
Cholesterol (mg)	0
Sodium (mg)	47
Potassium (mg)	201
Vitamin C (mg)	10
Vitamin E	

Preheat oven to 425°. Lightly spray a 10-inch pie pan with fat-free cooking spray. Set aside. Stack phyllo between 2 sheets of plastic wrap and cover with a damp kitchen towel. Center 1 phyllo sheet over pan and brush with 2 tablespoons of the apricot nectar. Top with a second phyllo sheet and brush with remaining 2 tablespoons of apricot nectar. Sprinkle chopped almonds over second sheet and top with remaining phyllo sheet. Carefully roll edge of phyllo sheets toward rim of pan to form a rigid edge. Press down. Bake pie shell on a baking sheet in the middle of oven until golden, about 4 minutes. Cool. In a small bowl, dissolve gelatin in water. Microwave on full power for 40 seconds until liquefied. Set aside. Drain tofu in a sieve-lined bowl for 10 minutes. Discard water and put tofu and sugar into a blender container. Blend mixture until soft and creamy. Add dissolved gelatin and almond extract and blend until well combined. Spoon into prepared pie crust. Evenly spread filling with a spatula. Arrange apricot slices around perimeter of the pie shell, working toward center. Strew blueberries over apricots. Brush fruit with softened apricot preserves. Serve immediately or refrigerate for no more than 6 hours. Cut into 8 wedges to serve.

VARIATION Substitute fresh strawberries, strawberry nectar and strawberry jam for the apricots, apricot nectar and jam.

OLD-FASHIONED BROWN RICE PUDDING

Slow baking gives this nostalgic rice pudding a creamy texture. Nutritious brown rice adds a crunchy nut-like quality.

1 can (12 ounces)
   evaporated nonfat milk

2 cups nonfat milk

½ cup water

⅓ cup sugar

½ teaspoon salt

2 teaspoons vanilla extract

¼ cup uncooked brown rice

1 cup raisins

MAKES 6 SERVINGS

nutritional analysis per serving

Calories (kcal) 218.4
Total Fat (g) 0.6
Cholesterol (mg) 4
Sodium (mg) 289
Potassium (mg) 526
Vitamin C (mg) 2

Preheat oven to 300°. In a large casserole dish, combine evaporated milk, milk, water, sugar, salt, vanilla and rice. Bake uncovered for 3 hours. During the first hour, stir 3 times with a fork so that the rice does not settle. After the first hour, stir in raisins. Continue baking until top is brown and a skin has formed. Remove from oven, cool slightly and serve.

TOFU BREAD PUDDING

Tofu blends with nonfat milk and Grand Marnier in this elegant bread pudding. Serve warm or at room temperature.

1 cup raisins

½ cup Grand Marnier

1 can (12 ounces) evaporated nonfat milk

1 cup nonfat milk

2 cups silken tofu, pureed with a blender

1 tablespoon grated orange zest

7 cups cubed French bread

fat-free cooking spray

4 egg whites

¾ cup sugar

2 teaspoons vanilla extract

1 teaspoon cinnamon

½ teaspoon nutmeg

MAKES 8 SERVINGS

nutritional analysis per serving

Calories (kcal)	841.8
Total Fat (g)	8.9
Cholesterol (mg)	2
Sodium (mg)	1359
Potassium (mg)	650
Vitamin C (mg)	3

Soak raisins in Grand Marnier until plump. Set aside. Combine evaporated milk, nonfat milk, half of the pureed tofu, orange zest and bread cubes. Stir well and set aside for about 30 minutes, or until bread absorbs liquid. Preheat oven to 375º. Lightly spray a 3-quart soufflé dish with fat-free cooking spray. Measure ¼ cup of the Grand Mariner from raisin mixture and set aside. Pour remaining raisin mixture into pudding mixture and stir. In a separate bowl, using an electric mixer, whip together egg whites until soft peaks form. Add ½ cup of the sugar and vanilla until blended. Gently fold egg white mixture into pudding mixture and pour into prepared soufflé dish. In a small bowl, mix together cinnamon, nutmeg and 2 tablespoons of the sugar. Sprinkle mixture over the top of the pudding. Bake until top is brown and puffy and center is firm, about 1 hour. Blend together remaining ¼ cup of Grand Marnier, remaining 2 tablespoons of sugar and remaining half of tofu puree. Remove pudding from oven and pour sauce over top. Spoon into dishes and serve.

VARIATION   To change the flavor of this delightful bread pudding, try using dark rum, whiskey, Cointreau, anisette or fruit brandies. Use left-over specialty breads such as pannetone, challah or brioche instead of French bread for a different flavor. Keep in mind that egg-enriched breads increase the amount of fat and cholesterol.

HAZELNUT MACAROONS

Macaroons are a natural low-fat dessert because of the egg whites. Hazelnuts are replaced with coconut and the amount of sugar is reduced without any loss of flavor or texture. Be sure not to overbake these macaroons; they should be very chewy.

parchment paper
2 egg whites
¼ teaspoon salt
¾ cup sugar
1 teaspoon hazelnut liqueur
2 cups ground hazelnuts

nutritional analysis per serving (2 macaroons)

Calories (kcal)	172.3
Total Fat (g)	12.0
Cholesterol (mg)	0
Sodium (mg)	54
Potassium (mg)	94
Vitamin C (mg)	0

MAKES 2 DOZEN MACAROONS

Preheat oven to 350°. Line a baking sheet with parchment paper and set aside. Beat egg whites until foamy. Gradually beat in salt and sugar until mixture thickens and becomes stiff. Fold in liqueur and hazelnuts. Use 2 teaspoons to shape batter into small mounds. Place mounds 2 inches apart on prepared baking sheet. Bake until set, about 10 to 15 minutes.

VARIATION   Substitute ground blanched almonds and almond extract for the hazelnuts and hazelnut liqueur.

BAKLAVA
Several changes are made in the classic baklava for this low-fat version. This recipe uses fruit nectar instead of butter to moisten the phyllo, honey instead of sugar for the syrup and cinnamon for flavor. Orange flower water, available in Middle Eastern stores, adds an exotic touch. Enjoy without guilt.

2 cups walnuts
½ teaspoon cinnamon
3 tablespoons orange flower
    water
¾ cup honey
fat-free cooking spray
⅔ cup pear nectar
½ pound phyllo dough
1 cup water
1 tablespoon lemon juice

MAKES 30 PIECES

nutritional analysis per serving (2 pieces)	
Calories (kcal)	205.1
Total Fat (g)	10.3
Cholesterol (mg)	0
Sodium (mg)	75
Potassium (mg)	110
Vitamin C (mg)	4

Preheat oven to 400°. Lightly coat a 9 x 13 baking pan with fat-free cooking spray. Grind walnuts by pulsing with a food processor for 50 seconds. Do not grind into a powder. Transfer to a small bowl. Stir in cinnamon, 1 tablespoon of the orange flower water and 1 tablespoon of the honey and set aside. In a cup, mix together 3 tablespoons of the honey with pear nectar. Set aside. Working quickly, unfold 3 phyllo sheets. Cover remaining sheets with plastic wrap and a damp towel. Spread 3 sheets on the bottom of the baking pan. Moisten with honey-pear mixture. Evenly spread walnut mixture over the pastry. Continue layering and brushing pastry with nectar mixture until all sheets are used. With your hands, press down pastry to compress. Cut baklava all the way through with a sharp knife, forming diamond-shaped pieces. Bake until golden, about 25 minutes. Remove from the oven and place on a wire rack to cool. In a small pan over medium heat, simmer water and remaining ½ cup honey until well dissolved. Remove from heat and stir in lemon juice. Cool slightly and add remaining 1 tablespoon of orange flower water. Spoon syrup over baklava, recut the pieces and soak in syrup for several hours before serving.

Biscotti

Egg white keeps the cholesterol down in these traditional twice-baked cookies from Prato, Italy. Vary the flavor by substituting anise seeds and extract for the almonds. Enjoy dipping into cappuccino, Vin Santo from Tuscany or a late harvest muscatel from California.

parchment paper
3½ cups all-purpose flour
2 cups sugar
5 egg whites
1 teaspoon baking powder
¼ teaspoon salt
2 teaspoons vanilla extract
1 cup coarsely chopped
    toasted almonds

Makes 30 biscotti

nutritional analysis per serving (2 biscotti)

Calories (kcal)	1262.0
Total Fat (g)	39.2
Cholesterol (mg)	0
Sodium (mg)	604
Potassium (mg)	873
Vitamin C (mg)	0
Vitamin E	

Thirty minutes before baking, preheat oven to 350°. Line a 15-inch-long baking sheet with parchment paper and set aside. On a clean working surface, mound flour and make a well in the center. Place sugar, 4 egg whites, baking powder, salt and vanilla into the well. Gradually work flour into ingredients within well. Mix with your hands until smooth. If dough is too crumbly, add a little warm water. Knead in almonds, working the dough until almonds are incorporated, about 5 minutes. Shape dough into an oval disc. Seal with plastic wrap and refrigerate for 30 minutes. Cut chilled dough lengthwise in half. Roll each half into a log about 3 inches in diameter. Place logs 3 inches apart on a prepared baking sheet and flatten slightly. Beat 1 remaining egg white and brush on tops of dough logs. Bake for 35 minutes. Remove from oven and reduce temperature to 300°. Slightly cool logs. With a serrated knife, cut logs diagonally into 1-inch slices. Place cut side up on the baking sheets and bake an additional 15 minutes. Cool on racks and store in air-tight tins.

CHERRIES FLAMBÉ WITH FROZEN YOGURT

Flavorful sour Morello cherries make an easy, festive dessert.

1 jar (24 oz) sour Morello
  cherries in light syrup
¼ cup brandy
1 quart vanilla-flavored frozen
  yogurt

MAKES 4 SERVINGS

nutritional analysis per serving

Calories (kcal) 337.0
Total Fat (g) 8.3
Cholesterol (mg) 3
Sodium (mg) 131
Potassium (mg) 556
Vitamin C (mg) 7

Drain syrup from cherries and place syrup in a small saucepan. Set aside. Pit cherries and add to saucepan. Heat over medium-high and bring to a boil. Remove from heat and pour into a heat-resistant serving dish. Immediately pour in brandy, ignite and bring to the table flaming. Serve flaming cherries over frozen yogurt.